Implementing and Configuring SAP Global Trade Services

 **PRESS**

SAP PRESS is issued by
Bernhard Hochlehnert, SAP AG

SAP PRESS is a joint initiative of SAP and Galileo Press. The know-how offered by SAP specialists combined with the expertise of the publishing house Galileo Press offers the reader expert books in the field. SAP PRESS features first-hand information and expert advice, and provides useful skills for professional decision-making.

SAP PRESS offers a variety of books on technical and business related topics for the SAP user. For further information, please visit our website: *www.sap-press.com*.

Marc Hoppe
Inventory Optimization with SAP
2006, 480 pp.
ISBN 1-59229-097-3

Martin Murray
Understanding the Logistics Information System
approx. 325 pp.
ISBN 1-59229-108-2
November 2006

Roland Fischer
Business Planning with SAP SEM
2005, 403 pp.
ISBN 1-59229-033-7

Ulli Hoffman
Web Dynnpro for ABAP
2006, 360 pp.
ISBN 1-59229-078-7

Jitendra Singh

Implementing and Configuring SAP Global Trade Services

Galileo Press

Bonn • Boston

ISBN 1-59229-096-5

ISBN 13 978-1-59229-096-3

1st edition 2007

Editor Jawahera Saidullah
Copy Editor Nancy Etscovitz, UCG, Inc., Boston, MA
Cover Design Silke Braun
Layout Design Vera Brauner
Production Steffi Ehrentraut
Typesetting Typographie & Computer, Krefeld
Printed and bound in Germany

© 2007 by Galileo Press

SAP PRESS is an imprint of Galileo Press,

Boston (MA), USA

Bonn, Germany

Contents at a Glance

Contents

6   Risk Management 161

7   Miscellaneous Issues 179

Appendix 193

This chapter introduces SAP Global Trade Services (GTS) and its place in a corporation's suite of enterprise applications. We will also look at the various modules that make up SAP GTS and at business trends and imperatives for implementing this application.

1   Introduction to SAP Global Trade Services

1.1   Overview of SAP Global Trade Services

In today's world, companies have to trade internationally to reach new customers and new sources of supply. In doing so, they have to deal with international trade laws and regulations that they wouldn't have to deal with domestically. For instance, if your company wants to sell its products to an overseas customer, it has to make sure it has the requisite licenses from the appropriate regulatory authorities to do so. After it secures the licenses, it has to declare shipments to the customs authorities on the export and import sides of the transaction. Your company might also have to make declarations to its customers of the preference eligibility of your products under trade-preference agreements.

Global Trade Services (GTS) is a standalone application software from SAP. It is SAP's answer to the complexities of managing foreign-trade functions in a corporation. It helps a corporation manage the whole gamut of international trade functions such as compliance with licensing laws, logistics functions such as printing trade documents, and management of company activities in various preference agreements, e.g. the North American Free Trade Agreement (NAFTA) and the European Union (EU).

This book will introduce you to the various modules in GTS, as well as to the trade laws and principles behind the functionality. For each module, this book will delve progressively deeper into the configuration required to enable it and steps for using the functionality in day-to day trade transactions. The examples and screen shots incorporated in this book are from a GTS 3.0 system but it will remain valid till the next release, GTS 7.0. This book is useful for project team members implementing GTS, and for introducing IT team members and trade compliance and logistics personnel to the foreign trade principles and to the GTS application software.

SAP GTS runs on the SAP NetWeaver technology stack. This is the underlying technology for all SAP applications, including R/3 Enterprise, mySAP ERP, mySAP CRM, and mySAP SCM. GTS furthers the stated direction of SAP to pull application areas out of their monolithic ERP application, SAP R/3, and give them new homes in standalone applications. GTS does the same for the Foreign Trade sub-module within the Sales and Distribution module of R/3. SAP incorporated a lot of the functions of the foreign trade module that exists in R/3 and then improved them in GTS.

Within an enterprise, SAP GTS can function as a central engine for all foreign trade related business processes. Because it is built on the SAP NetWeaver technology, it can provide those foreign trade services to any third- party application and not just to SAP R/3. Naturally, the integration with SAP R/3 is much easier to set up than with other applications.

Example

A major high-tech company used best-in-class solutions for ERP and CRM from two different vendors. This heterogeneous application environment posed a risk from an export compliance perspective, for example by duplicating compliance rules in the two applications, and giving two different answers for the sanctioned-party-list screening function for the same customer. GTS as a standalone application offered a solution to this problem by integrating effectively with both applications and enabling the export-compliance managers to do their jobs from this one central application

1.2 SAP Global Trade Services Modules

SAP GTS comprises three distinct modules, as illustrated in Figure 1.1. These modules, which focus on specific foreign-trade processes, are given below:

► Compliance management

► Customs management

► Risk management

Besides sharing some master data, the modules are fairly independent of each other and serve disparate foreign trade needs within a company. Let us now get a more detailed understanding of each module.

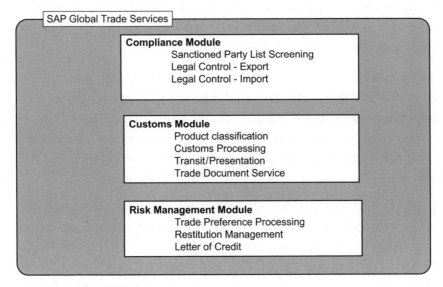

Figure 1.1 SAP Global Trade Services Modules

1.2.1 Compliance Management

The Compliance management module comprises three distinct sub-modules. These are:

► Sanctioned Party List Screening

► Legal Control Export

► Legal Control Import

Keep in mind that Legal Control Export and Legal Control Import have been combined for our discussion. Now let us examine these sub-modules in more detail.

Sanctioned Party List Screening (SPL)

This sub-module focuses on compliance with government laws that prohibit dealing with parties (individuals and organizations) that are sanctioned by various governmental agencies of countries where a company does business. From time to time, various government agencies come up with additions or deletions of names of individuals or companies that are sanctioned. Specifically, in the U.S. the Department of Commerce's Bureau of Industry and Security publishes the Denied Parties list, the Department of Treasury publishes the Specially Designated Nationals list, and the Department of State publishes the Debarred Persons list.

Companies operate in various countries and have to comply with the export laws of those countries even if their primary base of operations is elsewhere. Export-control laws have an extraterritorial nature; for example, a U.S. company operating in the UK needs to conform to all U.S. compliance laws designed to prevent dealings with sanctioned parties and vice versa.

The SPL screening sub-module enables screening of all customers, vendors, employees, and entities engaged in purely financial transactions against lists published by various agencies. It also enables real-time checks of business transactions such as sales orders, deliveries, and purchase orders to make sure the parties involved are not on any denied-party lists. The system lets you do the following:

▶ Upload aggregated lists from data providers such as MK Technologies Inc.

▶ Interface to non-R/3 back-end systems for SPL screening

▶ Enable real-time synchronous as well as asynchronous batch screening

▶ Block suspected partners and documents for human evaluation

▶ Audit block removals by keeping a detailed log of all activity

Legal Control Export/Import

These two sub-modules use essentially the same functions, so, depending on whether you are dealing with export or import, we can discuss them together. Legal Control Export/Import includes the Embargo Check function and the Export/Import license-management functions which are examined below.

▶ **Embargo Check**

The Embargo Check function helps comply with restrictions on doing business with certain countries. Government agencies and the United Nations can prohibit trade with certain countries. These embargoes mandate that no business dealings can be initiated with those countries. This module facilitates embargo checks by making sure none of the parties involved in a business transaction are in an embargo situation. The system lets you block suspect partners and documents. It also lets you audit block removals by keeping a detailed log of all activities. In addition, you can embargo exports from certain countries to an embargoed nation while letting trade flow from other countries

▶ **License Determination Export/Import**

Most countries maintain license regimes that mandate export or import of certain types of products under licenses from controlling government agencies. These license requirements apply to both finished goods and also to any kind of raw materials. They are intended to control exports to certain countries, or certain customers. There maybe varied reasons for control, for example those involving armaments and weapons, sensitive technology, or dual-use products.

Export license requirements are governed by the destination country, end customer, and by the Export Control Classification Number (ECCN) of the product. For instance in the U.S., the Department of Commerce publishes the ECCNs on the Commerce Control list, while the licensing requirements may be dictated by the Department of Commerce, Department of State, Food and Drug Administration, or Drug Enforcement Administration. This is a simplistic explanation of the process; a more nuanced discussion will follow in detail, covering issues such as re-export from destination country, final end use, tangible vs. intangible exports, and the functionality GTS offers to manage this process.

The Export Control module provides robust functionality to maintain the requirements dictated by the laws that you have to observe. With a combination of master data and license-determination rules, it checks all shipments to make sure they comply with the export-licensing laws of the country you operate in. This module lets you maintain licenses obtained from the authorities, applies them to sales orders, purchase orders, and deliveries based on predefined rules, and keeps track of quantities or value limits if needed. Non-compliant documents are blocked with a detailed log available for record keeping and subsequent audits.

The Import Control part of the Compliance module differs from the Export Control part in that it is governed by the departure country as opposed to the destination country. It shares the master data and determination rules with Export Control and can be selectively activated for certain departure countries as required.

1.2.2 Customs Management

The Customs Management module is devoted to trade functions that involve the actual flow of goods across borders. This includes communication with the customs authorities electronically and via the printing of standard forms required for customs clearance. The customs module includes the following:

- Product Classification
- Customs Processing
- Transit/Presentation
- Trade Document Service

Now let us take a closer look at these.

Product Classification

The product classification functionality in GTS facilitates assigning commodity codes, tariff codes, and export control classification numbers to products involved in exports and imports. Some of these codes are then used in making declarations to customs authorities. The purpose of the commodity codes is to identify the product to customs authorities using a common nomenclature without having them learn a company's product codes and understand what kind of product is involved.

This functionality facilitates the import of Harmonized Tariff Schedule (HTS) and Commodity codes in an XML file from external data providers such as FedEx Trade Networks. This simplifies the task of assigning the right codes and keeping up to date with any changes. Phonetic search through commodity code descriptions provides a user-friendly way of classifying products. However, the task of determining which is the right code for your product is still done manually. This functionality is crucial for the smooth movement of goods across borders and for the calculation of import duties paid by your company. The HTS codes are the basis for calculating import duties by customs; therefore their accuracy is very important.

> **Note**
>
> HTS is an international system of describing products through the use of a 10-digit code. The first six digits represent the chapter, heading, and sub-heading of the schedule and, with the last four digits, represent the complete commodity code. The first six digits are common across countries that use this system, while the last four digits can vary.

Customs Processing

This sub-module assists in making declarations of exports and imports to customs authorities using electronic messages and calculation of customs duties on imports. This helps increase the overall velocity of your supply chain by eliminating slower paper-based processes. SAP GTS is capable of communicating electronically with the customs authorities of a number of countries. Below is a short list of specific countries' customs IT systems with which GTS can communicate.

▶ **Automated Export System (AES)**
This applies to the U.S, and is used for declaring exports instead of making paper Shipper Export Declarations (SED). This will ultimately be supplanted by another system in the U.S., called Automated Commercial Environment (ACE).

▶ **Automated Tariff and Local Customs Clearance System (ATLAS)**
This is used in Germany and is an IT procedure that allows authorized consignees to replace paper-based declarations with electronic messages. Using the customs processing functionality involves maintaining the following:

▸ Products to be declared in GTS

▸ Assignment of commodity codes to those products

▸ Customs offices you want to declare to

▸ Business partners involved in the trade

▸ Customs duty rates

Creating the customs shipment for declaration can be either manually initiated in GTS or can be a document replicated from your back-end ERP system. The Customs Communication Service functionality then transfers the electronic declaration to customs and can process confirmation responses back from customs, if required.

Transit/Presentation

The fundamental Customs Communication Service functionality also drives the Transit/Presentation business process. This allows electronic communication with customs systems such as the European Union New Computerized Transit system (NCTS). The primary advantage of systems like NCTS is the ability to electronically pre-declare transit of goods, receiving goods directly at your premises for authorized consignees without any wait at customs offices. SAP GTS enables communications with these systems every step of the way. Having a robust IT infrastructure is one of the conditions for participating as an authorized consignor or consignee on the NCTS.

Trade Document Service

This functionality is geared towards print documents required for clearing customs. Standard documents such as the U.S. Shippers Export Declaration, Certificate of Origin, Shipper's Letter of Instruction, etc. are pre-delivered for use. You can configure the system to propose documents required for a specific customs situation. The process involves creating a customs shipment document in GTS or replicating an invoice document from the R/3 back-end system to a customs shipment document in GTS. The appropriate documents can either be printed on demand or in batch mode. Using SAP NetWeaver Enterprise Portal technology, those very same documents can be made available to freight forwarders and customs brokers through the Web.

From SAP Basis Release 6.40 onwards, the standard forms are available in Adobe format. This makes form printing and form modifications for compliance with regulatory changes, a lot easier.

1.2.3 Risk Management

The Risk Management module enables trade processes that deal with financial risk to your company. Specifically, preference processing within foreign trade zones like NAFTA and restitution under the EU Common Agricultural Policy (CAP). This module includes the following:

▶ Trade Preference Processing
▶ Restitution Handling

Let us now get a better understanding of both these sub-modules.

Trade Preference Processing

This sub-module enables you to benefit from preferential duties levied on goods with high content from within a trading bloc. Examples from NAFTA and the EU are reduced duties on goods manufactured with a high local content from within the member countries. This requires up-to-date maintenance of declarations from your suppliers certifying the percentage of local content. It also requires application of rules to determine the origin of your finished product, taking into account all the declarations for supplier materials that go into the bill of material (BOM). To facilitate this process, the system does the following:

▶ Lets suppliers make declarations on your system via the Web
▶ Sends notification to suppliers to update their declarations
▶ Enables XML file upload of preference calculation rules from data providers
▶ Keeps a detailed log of origin determination of your product
▶ Lets you maintain declarations needed by your customers

Restitution Handling

This sub-module enables you to seek refunds from government authorities for exports that qualify for direct subsidies. Specifically, this functionality is relevant for exports of agricultural or food products from EU to non-EU countries under Common Agricultural Policy (CAP). The process involves tendering a financial guarantee and applying for a license to export a certain quantity of goods. The next step is processing exports of those goods and calculation of restitution based on EU rules and ingredients in those products. Finally come filing of a refund application and tracking payment from the government.

To enable this process, the system does the following:

▶ Lets you maintain financial securities to be tendered
▶ Maintains licenses with validities and quantities
▶ Maintains recipes for processed food products
▶ Calculates refunds on export documents from your back-end ERP system
▶ Files refund application
▶ Invoices the refund in your back-end financial system to track payment

This concludes our introduction to the various GTS modules and their functionality. From the introduction, it is evident that GTS offers a breadth of modules that enable a number of trade processes. In the next section, we will discuss the regulatory trends and business environment that favor GTS.

1.3   Global Trade Trends and SAP GTS

Many trends impact the execution of global trade. These trends have made it more complex and risky to falter in execution. Some of these trends are regulatory in nature, such as the Sarbanes Oxley Act, while some are the result of changes in the global business environment, such as globalization of the supply chain. Let's see how these trends operate in the real world.

1.3.1   Regulatory Trends

The regulatory trend most talked about these days is the Sarbanes-Oxley Act and the changes brought about by the U.S. Homeland Security initiatives.

Sarbanes Oxley Act

The Sarbanes-Oxley Act of 2002 (SOX) is perhaps the most far-reaching legislation aimed at public companies. Although the focus of the act is on improving financial disclosure so as to protect investors, it has implications for operational controls and global trade management, and these in turn have an impact on a company's financials. Section 404 of SOX mandates company executives to certify the effectiveness of internal controls including procedures for denied-party screening, license determination, tariff classification, and preferential trade agreements, all of which are functions supported by GTS.

Compliance with this act has required companies to remake their internal controls. GTS can enable remaking of the controls specific to the global supply chain, so as to reduce the risk and improve reliability of these processes.

Homeland Security

In the wake of the 9/11 terrorist attacks, the U.S. government passed the Patriot Act, which has resulted in a number of U.S. customs initiatives that have profound implications for global trade. These initiatives have resulted in tightening of border controls, more onerous customs declaration requirements, tighter export licensing of dual-use products, and other actions.

A number of U.S. customs initiatives such as Customs-Trade Partnership Against Terrorism (C-TPAT), Container Security Initiative (CSI), and Fast and Secure Trade (FAST) have the intent of identifying certified importers, exporters, carriers and their goods as low risk and hence requiring less inspection. However, most of these programs work in conjunction with participation in the Automated Commercial Environment (ACE). This means the importer or carrier needs to electronically pre-declare the incoming shipment to be considered low-risk, and that's where an application like SAP GTS can help.

1.3.2 Globalization of the Supply Chain Trend

In an increasingly smaller world, the supply chain has become global, spread out across boundaries. This trend is important to take note of when talking about the trends affecting GTS. Let's look at the major aspects of this trend.

Manufacturing Outsourcing/JIT Supply Chain

The globalization of the supply chain resulting from either manufacturing outsourcing or from companies moving operations to lower-cost countries poses an operational challenge. A supply chain that's fragmented across different countries and one that relies on just-in-time (JIT) supply process makes timely customs clearance a critical operational need. SAP GTS is an enabler for the global supply chain with its certified communications with the customs authorities of a number of countries. Overall, it contributes to improving the supply chain velocity by assuring data quality and electronic declarations to authorities.

Trade Preference Agreements

Another trend driving the adoption of a global trade management application like SAP GTS is the proliferation of trade preference agreements such as those used by NAFTA, the EU, and the Association of South East Asian Nations (ASEAN). These agreements benefit member countries by lowering the tariffs paid on goods movements within the trade bloc on products with more than specified local content. Complicated rule sets for claiming reduced tariffs and certifying origin of the products require the use of an enabler like SAP GTS.

1.4 SAP R/3 Foreign Trade and GTS

Most SAP customers evaluating SAP GTS are SAP R/3 customers that have implemented the Foreign Trade sub-module within the Sales and Distribution module in SAP R/3. It is instructive to talk about the differences and advantages of introducing SAP GTS as a replacement for the Foreign Trade module. Let's talk about the migration path that SAP offers for SAP R/3 customers to be able to implement SAP GTS, as well as the improvements and the tools that can help drive adoption.

The Foreign Trade sub-module in SAP R/3 has some limited functionality to enable export compliance and trade preference processing. SAP GTS builds upon that capability and makes it considerably more powerful.

1.4.1 Improvements in GTS

GTS improves over the equivalent R/3 Foreign Trade functionality in numerous ways, including partnering with third-party data provider companies that provide XML files of master data that is published by government agencies; e.g. export license determination rules, SPL lists, or ECCN lists. Using XML files significantly reduces the effort required by GTS customers to keep up with changes to this data, transferring the burden to the data provider. In general there are several improvements in GTS that help alleviate the manual work necessitated in R/3. Improvements in GTS over R/3 Foreign Trade by module include:

Improvements in Export Compliance (Sanctioned Party List Screening)

▸ Synchronous checking of business partners and documents

▸ Ability to tune matching logic to achieve an acceptable rate of false positives

▸ Detailed audit logs of sanctioned list updates uploaded from data providers like MK Technologies

▸ Detailed logs of blocking and unblocking of documents and partners

▸ Address simulation capabilities

▸ Simulation of new updates from MK Technologies in a production environment

Improvements to Legal Control—Export and Import

▸ Quantity and value limits on export licenses

▸ Export-license check of certified customers for dual-use technology

▸ Flexibility on using any type of business partner (sold-to, ship-to etc.) to drive license determination

▶ Greater granularity in checking export license required for a shipment. License checks can be made in the following ways:

  ▶ Customer specific

  ▶ ECCN specific

  ▶ Destination-country specific

  ▶ Foreign trade-organization specific

  ▶ Sales-order specific

  ▶ Material specific

  ▶ Detailed audit logs of license block removals

  ▶ XML uploads of ECCN; HTS numbers from data providers such as FedEx Trade Networks

Improvements in Customs Management

Besides completely new functionality on Customs Communication Service, improvements on corresponding functionality in SAP R/3 include the following:

▶ XML Uploads of Customs duty rates from data providers

▶ Web access to customs forms for external partners like freight forwarders and subcontractors

▶ Pre-defined templates of customs forms, including:

  ▶ Pro forma invoices

  ▶ Certificate of Origin

  ▶ Shipper's letter of instruction

  ▶ Unloading and loading forms (EU)

  ▶ Paper Shippers Export Declaration

Improvements in Risk Management

The Risk Management module in GTS improves over corresponding functionality in R/3. The improvements in the each of the two sub-modules of Risk management are:

- ▶ Restitution Management
  - ▶ License Management for Restitution
  - ▶ Recipe maintenance for processed agriculture products to determine restitution
  - ▶ Ability to file and monitor refund requests for restitution
- ▶ Preference processing
  - ▶ Managing vendor declaration work lists
  - ▶ Creating vendor declaration for customers

Now that you have looked at some of the improvements in GTS over similar R/3 foreign trade modules, you may want to transfer your trade processes to GTS. Therefore, the next section talks about the migration path for R/3 customers looking to leverage GTS functionality.

1.4.2 Migration Path

The migration path is important for customers replacing their R/3 foreign trade functionality with GTS. SAP customers with R/3 Foreign Trade implemented already expended spent time and effort in doing so. Tools and utilities smooth the migration path to GTS by transferring existing data from R/3 to GTS in a systematic fashion, significantly reducing manual effort. SAP provided migration path consists of the following.

Compatibility with Older Releases of SAP R/3

Plug-in code in SAP R/3 is the middleware component that forms the technical underpinning of connecting to SAP GTS. All new-dimension products such as mySAP CRM and mySAP SRM use the same plug-in that GTS uses for connecting to the back-end R/3 systems. The plug-in itself is based on SAP's Remote Function Call (RFC) technology.

The plug-in enables the connection between releases of R/3 older than mySAP ERP to SAP GTS. It enables the transfer of business partners, materials, and documents from R/3 to GTS. Services like SPL screening or license determination are performed on the transferred document or partner and the results communicated back to SAP R/3 via the same RFC technology.

Tools for Transferring Data for Initial Implementation

An important component of the migration path from R/3 foreign trade sub-module to SAP GTS is the data-transfer technology. To assist with transferring data from the foreign trade module in SAP R/3 to GTS, a number of tools are available, as shown in Table 1.1.

Program Name	Purpose
/SAPSLL/ALNUM_UPLOAD_R3	Upload ECCN's (master list) from R/3
/SAPSLL/CCGR_UPLOAD_R3	Upload R/3 groupings used in license determination
/SAPSLL/CD01_UPLOAD_R3	Upload R/3 license determination rules to GTS
/SAPSLL/MAEX_UPLOAD_R3	Apply R/3 material master ECCN assignment to product master in GTS
/SAPSLL/MARC_UPLOAD_R3	Apply R/3 material master commodity code assignment to product master in GTS

Table 1.1 R/3 to-GTS Data Transfer Utilities

Besides the one-time use utilities, there are tools available on the R/3 side in the plug-in that enable the transfer of business partners, sales orders, deliveries, purchase orders, and invoice documents to SAP GTS.

1.5   Introduction to the GTS User Interface and Implementation Guide

SAP GTS is an SAP application, and it adheres to most of the principles of an SAP application. Examples include the concept of a table-driven configuration, the use of the SAP GUI to access the application, transaction codes, and menus that look very similar to SAP R/3. This helps in leveraging the combined knowledge that exists in companies that already use SAP R/3 or other SAP applications.

1.5.1   GTS User Interface

As you log in to SAP GTS, the main menu as shown in Figure 1.2 is accessed by transaction /SAPSLL/MENU_LEGAL. The menu mirrors the neat segregation of the application into three tracks: *Compliance, Customs,* and *Risk Management*.

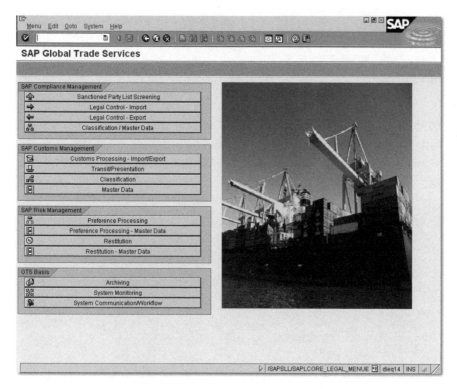

Figure 1.2 SAP GTS Application Menu

Note

As in any other SAP application, a user can be set up for different default menu transactions. For instance, a logistics person may only be interested in customs transactions and can be set to default transaction SAPSLL/MENU_CUS. Similarly, for SPL screening the transaction would be SAPSLL/MENU_SPL. Setting up the users with the default transaction presents them with their subset of SAP GTS on login.

All GTS application transactions and program names exist in the /SAPSLL namespace. This is how SAP segregates the GTS-specific application programs from the general infrastructure programs. There are two ways of accessing GTS functions. You can use the menu paths as shown in Figure

1.2. Or you can directly access the functions via the transaction code in the command line, as shown in Figure 1.3.

Figure 1.3 SAP GUI Command Line Access to Transactions

To find out the transaction code being used on any transaction, use menu path **System • Status** to see the details illustrated in Figure 1.4. For instance, you can see in Figure 1.4, that the transaction is SAPSLL/PR_PRCON_02.

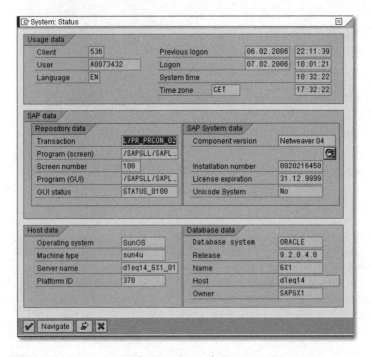

Figure 1.4 System Status Showing Currently Executing Transaction

For help with a field on any screen, put your cursor in that field and press **<F1>** on your keyboard. This triggers the Performance Assistant window with help on the meaning of the field (see Figure 1.5).

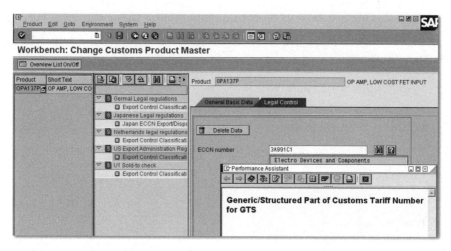

Figure 1.5 Field-Level Help Using F1 Key

1.5.2 Implementation Guide

GTS uses the Implementation Guide (IMG), as shown in Figure 1.6, to customize and adapt the application to specific business scenarios. Every company that implements GTS has different needs and business processes. In order to customize SAP GTS to those processes, the implementation team has to go through the process of configuration. The IMG is the place where you configure SAP GTS. A series of steps in this guide lets you tweak it according to your needs.

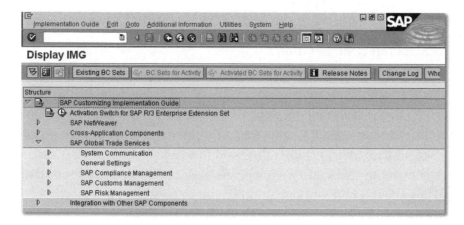

Figure 1.6 SAP GTS Implementation Guide

Most of this book will focus on the Implementation Guide shown in Figure 1.6. The implementation guide is organized into five main tracks, which are listed below:

▸ System Communication, which focuses on the setting up of the middle-ware connection between SAP R/3 or any other feeder system and SAP GTS

▸ General Settings, which covers the Organization Structure setup

▸ Compliance Management

▸ Customs Management

▸ Risk Management

Now that you have had a brief introduction to the GTS menus, user interface and the implementation guide, we will talk about GTS implementation in the context of SAP's ASAP implementation methodology.

1.6   Implementing SAP GTS with ASAP methodology

Accelerated SAP or ASAP is the roadmap from SAP for implementing its applications. It is a distillation of experiences from various SAP implementations. This methodology provides an exhaustive list of tasks relevant for the various phases of an implementation. These phases are examined in the sub-sections that follow.

1.6.1   Project Preparation

In this phase, you would organize your implementation team, determine how you want to implement GTS; in phases or as a big bang. You will also determine the landscape for your GTS system. Typically this would look simillar to your SAP R/3 landscape, with the sizing of your GTS system based on transaction volumes that need to be serviced. This phase essentially performs preliminary work before your implementation team starts talking about the specific functionality that you want to implement.

1.6.2 Business Blueprint and Realization

In this phase, you would create the technical design document. This document is the input for the realization phase and has all the information needed to start customizing the system using the implementation guide. For a GTS system, the business blueprint phase is when the project team decides on the answers to questions like the following:

▶ How many foreign trade organization to create in GTS?

▶ How to map company codes from R/3 to foreign trade organizations in GTS?

▶ What document types to transfer from R/3 to GTS?

▶ What services to perform on the transferred documents?

▶ Which partner types to transfer from R/3 to GTS?

▶ How many legal regulations to configure in GTS etc.?

1.6.3 Realization Phase

This phase involves actual customization of the system, development of any enhancements identified during the blueprint phase, and transfer to the quality-assurance environment.

1.6.4 Final Preparation

In this phase, you set up the production GTS system by transporting the customizaiton settings. You need to perform a final check of the system settings before the go-live. Performance testing is an important element of this phase. Since document creation and change in feeder R/3 systems await a response from GTS, robust system performance is key to a successful GTS implementation. Based on the checks in this phase, you can decide whether the system is ready for go-live.

1.6.5 Go Live and Support

This phase involves supporting the production GTS application. You would answer any questions from your user base and monitor the system to make sure it is behaving as designed. You need to perform system conversions ahead of time to transfer master data from feeder R/3 systems. Be sure to transfer customers, materials, vendors and open documents to GTS before the actual go-live.

1.7   Conclusion

In this chapter, we talked about SAP Global Trade Services and its various modules, the underlying principles of foreign trade, and the concept of a global trade management application like GTS, as well as its role in helping facilitate trade. We talked about the globalization challenges to business and how SAP GTS can help. We covered the roadmap for implementing SAP GTS for R/3 customers. In Chapter 2, we will delve into the first steps of implementing and configuring SAP GTS.

This chapter examines the configuration required for connecting SAP Global Trade Services (GTS) to an R/3 back-end system. We will cover both the technical communication setup and the organizational structure mapping. These activities are among the first steps when implementing GTS and laying the foundation for use by the various modules.

2 Implementing GTS with an R/3 Back-End System

Before we start our discussion on connecting GTS to an R/3 back end, it is instructive to note the fundamentals of how GTS works with any back-end system. Any service available in GTS can be performed either for business partners like customers and vendors or for business documents such as sales orders, deliveries, or billing documents. For any of these services to be performed on the documents, there are prerequisites that need to be met. For instance, for any document transferred to GTS from a back-end system, the business partners, and the materials involved in the document need to be already present in GTS. This means that the business partners and materials from the back-end system need to be replicated to GTS ahead of time. When the documents are created in the back-end system, they are transferred to GTS and the services configured are performed on those documents.

2.1 Setting Up System Communication in the R/3 Back End

Before your back-end system can start consuming the services that GTS offers, you need to set up the technical basis on which the two systems can talk to each other. Setting up the communication accomplishes the transfer of business partners and documents on which GTS services such as sanctioned party list (SPL) screening can be performed. GTS uses the concept of remote function calls (RFCs) to talk to the R/3 back-end system and vice versa. The connection between the two systems is based on SAP's Application link enabling (ALE) technology.

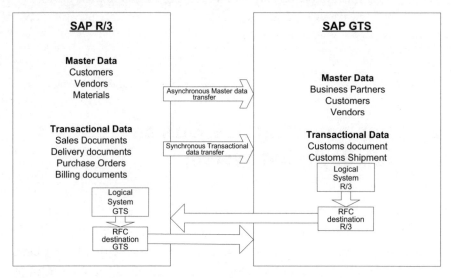

Figure 2.1 System Communication Between R/3 and GTS

As shown in Figure 2.1, master data such as customers, vendors, and materials are transferred asynchronously from the back-end R/3 system to GTS. Transactional data such as sales documents, delivery documents, and billing documents are transferred synchronously when they are saved in R/3. Implementation involves one-time mass transfer of master data and subsequent transfer of new and changed master data.

Within R/3 you can access transaction /SAPSLL/MENU_LEGALR3 as a portal to make all setups required for connecting to GTS. Use the following steps (see Figure 2.2):

1. Define your GTS system as a logical system (see Figure 2.3).

2. Define your GTS system as a RFC destination in the R/3 via transaction SM59 accessed from /SAPSLL/MENU_LEGALR3.

3. Associate the logical system for GTS with the RFC destination for GTS. This can be done using transaction BD97. Maintain RFC destination for Method Calls.

4. Assign the RFC destination for GTS to the logical system for GTS by
clicking on the **Standard RFC destination for BAPI Calls** function, as
shown in Figure 2.6.

Note

Transaction /SAPSLL/TBDLS_R3 is accessed from the R/3 transaction /SAPSLL/
MENU_LEGALR3 as shown in Figure 2.2.

Note

An RFC destination specifies the technical parameters for accessing GTS including the IP address of the system (see Figure 2.4) and the user and password (see
Figure 2.5) required for accessing GTS.

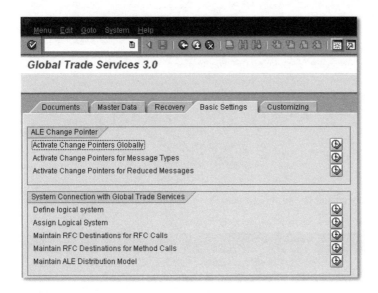

Figure 2.2 Basic Settings Tab of R/3 Transaction /SAPSLL/MENU_LEGALR3

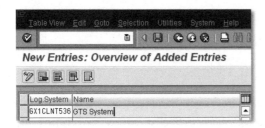

Figure 2.3 Defining GTS System as a Logical System in R/3

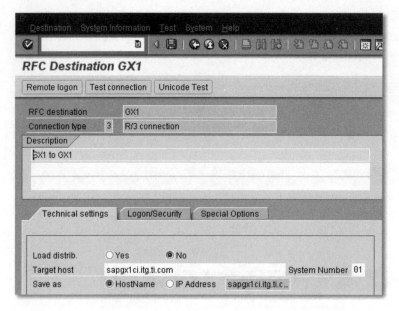

Figure 2.4 Transaction SM59 for Defining RFC Destination for GTS in R/3

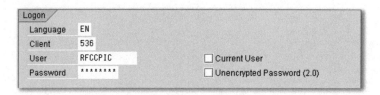

Figure 2.5 SM59 Logon Tab to Specify User and Password for Accessing GTS

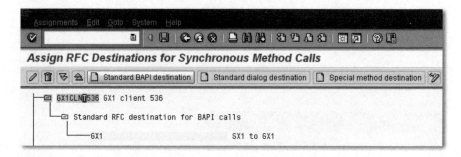

Figure 2.6 Assigning RFC Destination for Method Calls

Before you can transfer master data to GTS, you have to set up the ALE distribution model, shown in Figure 2.7. This model specifies the sending and receiving of logical systems and the message types that will be transferred.

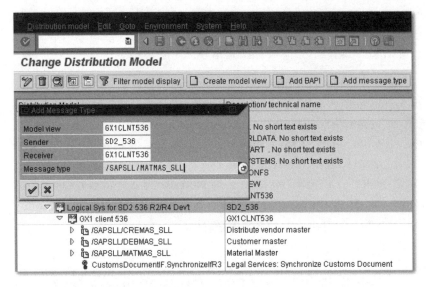

Figure 2.7 ALE Distribution Model

The sending logical system is the R/3 back-end system from which you are sending the data. The receiving logical system is the logical system name you gave to your GTS system. The message types that need to be transferred are in the /SAPSLL namespace and are given below:

- /SAPSLL/MATMAS_SLL – Material master
- /SAPSLL/DEBMAS_SLL – Customer master
- /SAPSLL/CREMAS_SLL – Vendor master

Now you need to turn on the change pointer for message types as shown in Figure 2.8, using transaction BD50. Turning on change pointers accomplishes subsequent transfer of master data from R/3 to GTS.

Figure 2.8 Turn on Change Pointer for GTS Message Types

Every time there is a change to a customer, material, or vendor, a change pointer is logged. Regularly scheduled batch jobs for program RBDMIDOC pick up these change pointers and push the objects to GTS.

The system also lets you develop reduced messages. These reduced messages log a change pointer only if certain elements of the material, customer, or vendor change. For instance, a change to the sales view of the customer is not relevant for transfer to GTS. Using transaction BD53, you can develop a reduced message from the /SAPSLL/DEBMAS message that does not include the sales-view data. This prevents needless transfers, by ensuring that every time the sales view of a customer changes the customer is not logged to be transferred to GTS again.

2.2 Setting up System Communication in GTS for a R/3 Back End

The first step in GTS is to define a logical system for the R/3 back-end system that will be connecting to GTS. Figure 2.9 shows the logical system definition for R/3 in GTS.

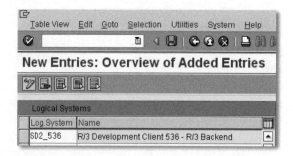

Figure 2.9 Logical System Definition for R/3 in GTS

Then you need to create the RFC destination for the R/3 system. Using transaction SM59, you can create the RFC destination. You then need to associate the RFC destination for R/3 with the logical system for R/3. This is done using transaction BD97, as shown in Figure 2.10. With this last step, the technical connection between R/3 and GTS is complete. You can now start configuring GTS.

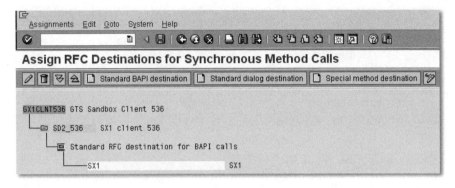

Figure 2.10 Associating RFC Destination for R/3 with Logical System Name for R/3 in GTS

2.3 GTS Organizational Structure

The organizational structure in GTS is created to reflect the way your company operates, the countries it operates in, and the customs laws that it needs to adhere to. The organizational structure from the back-end system is mapped to the organizational units in GTS. The two main units that define the structure in GTS are listed below:

▸ Foreign trade Organization

▸ Legal Unit

Now we can examine these in more detail.

2.3.1 Foreign Trade Organization

Foreign Trade Organization is the top-level unit to which company codes from the R/3 back end are assigned. You can assign more than one company code to the same foreign trade organization, but a company code can be assigned to at most one foreign trade organization. Foreign trade organizations are created as business partner with role SLLFTO in GTS, as shown in Figure 2.11. The customs declarations use it as the sender partner when communicating with customs; therefore, any company code with goods movement needs a matching foreign trade organization.

> **Note**
>
> Having multiple foreign trade organizations is useful for segmenting responsibilities in GTS. If your company has compliance and customs functions decentralized by—for instance—geography, you can assign all company codes in a given region to a single foreign trade organization. This also makes it easier to use the email and workflow functionality in GTS, by enabling by region user groups to be notified of problems pertaining only to their foreign trade organizations.

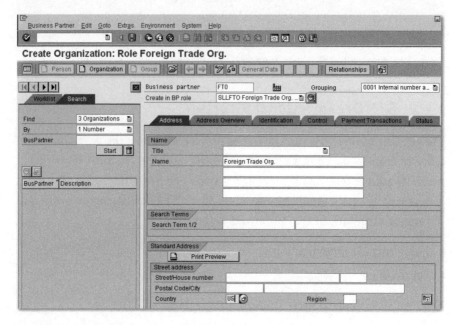

Figure 2.11 Foreign Trade Organization Creation

After creating the foreign trade organization, you need to assign company codes form the back-end R/3 system. This can be done from the implementation guide in GTS, using transaction SPRO as shown in Figure 2.12 and in Figure 2.13.

Figure 2.12 Implementation Guide for Creating and Assigning Foreign Trade Organization

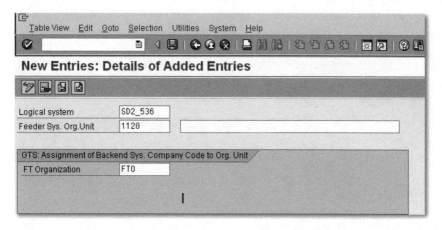

Figure 2.13 Assignment of Foreign Trade Organizations to Company Codes

If you have multiple back-end R/3 systems with the same organizational structure connected to GTS, you can map company codes to foreign trade organizations at the feeder system group level. This can be done by first creating a feeder system group and then by assigning the logical systems names of the R/3 systems to this group.

> **Note**
>
> If the system does not find the mapping for the company code in GTS, it cancels the saving of the document in the back-end R/3 system.

2.3.2 Legal Units

A legal unit is a GTS organizational unit that represents a stock ownership entity from the back-end R/3 system. Legal units further subdivide the foreign trade organization unit. Multiple legal units can be mapped to the same foreign trade organization, but a legal unit can be mapped to, at most, one foreign trade organization. Plants or combination of plants and storage locations from the R/3 back-end system are mapped to legal units in GTS. Just like foreign trade organizations, legal units are created as business partners in GTS. However, legal units are created in role **SLLSIT**, as shown in Figure 2.14.

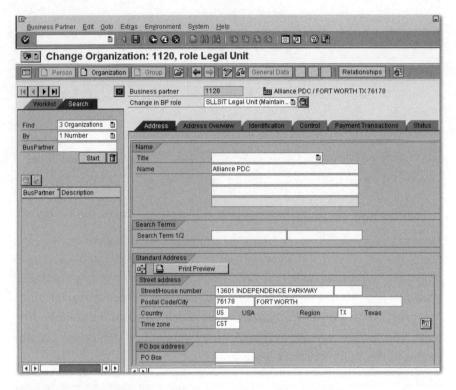

Figure 2.14 Legal Unit Creation

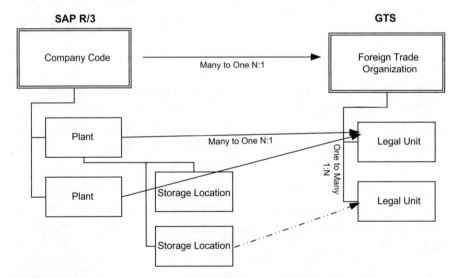

Figure 2.15 GTS Organizational Hierarchy Mapped to R/3 Organization Units

The country of the legal unit is used by the system to determine the country of departure in case of export orders and the country of destination for import orders. If in the back-end R/3 system you have a plant with storage locations that have different addresses, you will have to assign plant and storage location combination to a legal unit, as illustrated in Figure 2.15

After defining the legal units, you need to map them to the plant or plant and storage location combination from the back-end R/3 system as shown in Figure 2.16.

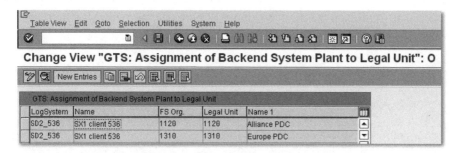

Figure 2.16 Assignment of R/3 Plant to Legal Unit in GTS

Note
If the system does not find mapping for the R/3 plant to the legal unit in GTS, it cancels the saving of the document in the back-end R/3 system.

The final step in maintaining the organization structure in GTS is to assign the legal units to foreign trade organizations.

Note
The organizational setup is shared by all the modules in GTS. The same organizational units and their relationships are used by the Compliance, Customs, and Risk Management modules.

2.4   Legal Regulations

Legal regulations are the controlling elements that determine the customs or compliance laws to be observed in GTS for business transactions executing in the back-end R/3 system.

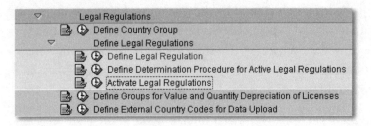

Figure 2.17 Legal Regulation Customizing in Transaction SPRO

In the definition of the legal regulation (see Figure 2.17), you can specify the country of origin of the laws that will be implemented using that legal regulation as shown in Figure 2.18. Every country whose laws your company must adhere to needs to have its own legal regulation.

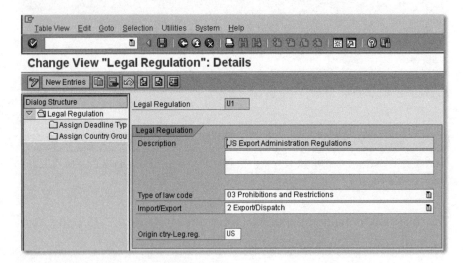

Figure 2.18 Legal Regulation Definition

Standard GTS offers six law codes to choose from (see Figure 2.19) when setting up the legal regulation. The choice of law code decides what services can be performed under that legal regulation. For example, law code **03 Prohibitions and Restrictions**—enables three services under the compliance function including SPL screening, embargo check, and license determination. You can read about these in Chapter 3.

00	German Foreign Trade Laws
01	Customs Processing
03	Prohibitions and Restrictions
06	Preference Law
07	Transit Process: Import/Export
08	Restitution
99	Others

Figure 2.19 Law Codes Available in GTS

2.4.1 Deadline Types

You can assign deadline types to the legal regulation as shown in Figure 2.20. The deadlines have different uses depending on the law code of the legal regulation. For instance, with SPL screening function, these deadlines specify the validity of the SPL records, while for license determination these deadlines specify the validity of the licenses.

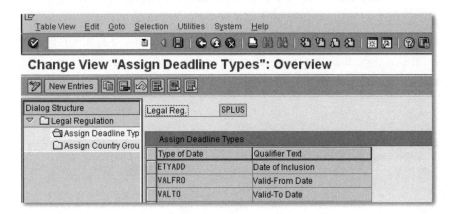

Figure 2.20 Deadline Types for a Legal Regulation

2.4.2 Country Groups

Country groups define groups of countries that have uniform requirements; e.g., license determination service can use country groups that have the same licensing requirements. This helps reduce the amount of master-data maintenance. Instead of specifying license requirements for each country separately, you specify them once, for all the countries in the country group.

Country groups can be specified as a part of the legal regulation definition as shown in Figure 2.21, but the assignment of countries to a country group is a master data function that can be accomplished using transaction /SAPSLL/CTYGPA

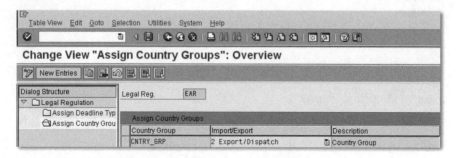

Figure 2.21 Assignment of Country Group to a Legal Regulation

2.4.3 Determination Procedures for Legal Regulations

Determination procedure (see Figure 2.22) specifies the determination strategy for the system to find the active legal regulations. For any GTS service, the system uses determination procedure assigned to that service to establish the determination strategy.

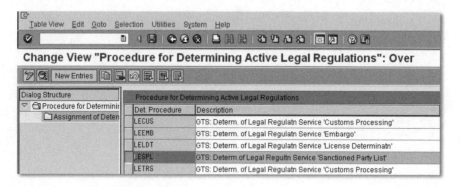

Figure 2.22 Determination Procedure

This strategy in turn tells the system how to identify the legal regulations that are active for that service. There is only one determination strategy, **Det. Procedure** available in GTS, as shown in Figure 2.23.

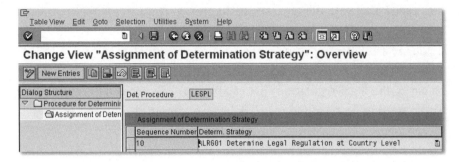

Figure 2.23 Assignment of Determination Strategy to a Procedure

2.4.4 Activation of Legal Regulations

Before legal regulations can be activated for a specific service in GTS, they need to be activated based on the determination strategy. Since there is only one determination strategy available as of GTS 7.0, which is at the country level, by default you need to activate that legal regulation for a country as shown in Figure 2.24.

Legal Reg.	Description	Ctry of Dep/Des	Name
TIEMB	Embargo Countries	NL	Netherlands
TIEMB	TI Embargo Countries	PH	Philippines
TIEMB	TI Embargo Countries	PT	Portugal
TIEMB	TI Embargo Countries	SE	Sweden
TIEMB	TI Embargo Countries	SG	Singapore
TIEMB	TI Embargo Countries	TH	Thailand
TIEMB	TI Embargo Countries	TW	Taiwan
TIEMB	TI Embargo Countries	US	USA
TISPL	Sanctioned Party List Legal Regulatio..	AU	Australia
TISPL	Sanctioned Party List Legal Regulatio..	BE	Belgium
TISPL	Sanctioned Party List Legal Regulatio..	BM	Bermuda
TISPL	Sanctioned Party List Legal Regulatio..	BR	Brazil
TISPL	Sanctioned Party List Legal Regulatio..	CA	Canada
TISPL	Sanctioned Party List Legal Regulatio..	CH	Switzerland

Figure 2.24 Legal Regulation Activation by Country

You need to activate the legal regulation for all countries where you want to observe the set of laws established by that legal regulation. For instance, if you are a U.S-based company, you are required by law to adhere to U.S. export licensing requirements no matter where you do business. In this scenario, the legal regulation that establishes U.S. licensing requirements would need to be activated for all departure countries.

2.5 Additional Requirements

Additional configuration requirements include assigning a time zone to the GTS system, maintaining number ranges for GTS objects like materials, documents, or licenses, and maintaining country codes used by external data providers different from the ISO country codes.

2.5.1 Maintain System Time Zone

System time zone determines the time stamp on the SPL records, customs documents, determination logs, etc. This is one of the first steps you need to take before you start using the system because the time stamps are used by the system to clearly indicate the date and times of the activity in question. This date and time in turn may influence the behavior of the system. This could happen if, for example, the date time stamp of the customs document is compared to the validity date and time of the SPL record to determine if the system should match against a SPL entity.

2.5.2 Maintain Number Ranges

Number ranges need to be maintained for a number of objects, such as business partners, product master, or customs documents, as shown in Figure 2.25. These number ranges are used by GTS to assign a GTS identification number to material master, customer, vendor, and documents coming from the back-end R/3 system.

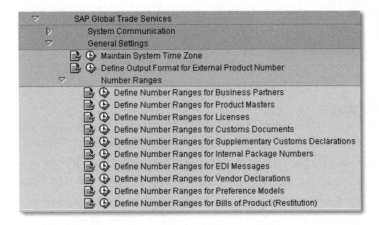

Figure 2.25 Number Range Maintenance in GTS Customizing

2.5.3 External Country Codes

External country codes can be set up to define additional codes that are used by data providers. For instance, Gaza is used by data providers to designate country information in SPL records. This functionality in GTS can be used to link **Gaza Strip** to the country code for **Israel**, as seen in Figure 2.26.

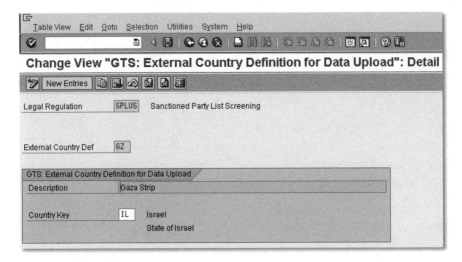

Figure 2.26 Assign External Country Codes for Data Providers

This concludes the discussion of settings required in GTS to connect to an R/3 back end and to set up an organizational structure that maps to the R/3 organizational structure.

2.6   Conclusion

In this chapter, we looked at the technical settings that enable an R/3 back-end system to talk to GTS. These technical settings are needed by the system to receive the master data and documents that consume the GTS trade services. We also described the organizational structure in GTS and how it maps to the organization units in R/3, and we discussed the importance of this mapping to the functioning of GTS services. We explained the concept of legal regulations central to the functioning of GTS.

To summarize, the technical settings for communication and the organization structure mapping between GTS and R/3 are the bedrock on which a back-end R/3 systems can take full advantage of the trade service offered in GTS. In Chapter 3, we will begin to explore the compliance services and their implementation in GTS.

In this chapter we will learn about the Compliance Management module, focusing specifically on the Sanctioned Party List screening services. We will cover the document structure in compliance and learn how it maps to the documents from R/3 back-end system.

3 Compliance Management—Part I

Government authorities in most countries lay down the laws that govern the export and import of tangible products, as well as intangible products such as intellectual property or technical know-how These authorities expect due diligence from businesses that enter into business transactions with foreign governments, entities, and naturalized persons. Failure to follow the law can result in fines, prison sentences for company executives, and suspension of export and import privileges. In the U.S., the Bureau of Industry and Security (BIS) under the Department of Commerce is the governing body for export transactions. It publishes the Export Administration Regulations that spell out the compliance laws to be followed by U.S.-based companies.

The BIS regularly publishes details of export-control violations that result in convictions, including names of executive officers of companies involved. It's in the interest of your company to have robust export compliance program, and this is where GTS can help.

The Compliance Management module in GTS specifically deals with the implementation of compliance laws of the country where you do business, to ensure that all business transactions entered into by your company are legitimate and lawful. As discussed in Chapter 1, compliance management consists of three main services, which are listed below:

- ▶ Sanctioned Party List (SPL) Screening
- ▶ Embargo Check
- ▶ License determination

These services are performed on business partners and on documents coming from back-end R/3 systems (see Figure 3.1). Every document that gets transferred from R/3 gets mapped to a GTS document.

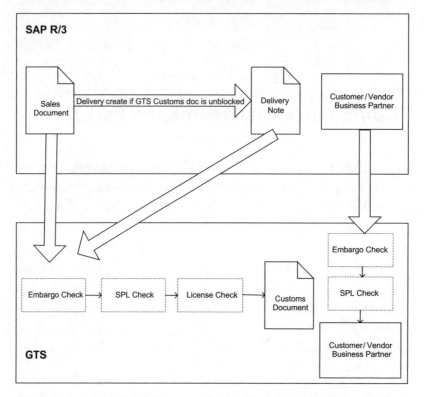

Figure 3.1 Compliance Check on Documents and Business Partners in GTS

3.1 Document Structure in GTS

The document structure in GTS borrows its main concepts from the SAP R/3 world. There are three main elements that constitute a document in GTS and how it behaves. These are listed below:

▸ Customs document type

▸ Customs item category

▸ Partner functions

Setting up the document structure in GTS involves creating the three previously identified elements and then mapping them to their counterparts from the R/3 back-end system. These activities can be accessed from the GTS implementation guide using transaction SPRO, as shown in Figure 3.2. Let's take a closer look at these elements now.

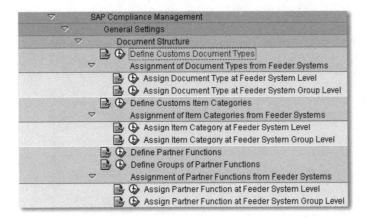

Figure 3.2 Setting Up Document Structures in GTS

3.1.1 Customs Document Type

This represents the type of customs document that is created in GTS when a back-end R/3 document is transferred. Customs document type is the identifier in GTS that corresponds to the document type from the R/3 back-end system. GTS is delivered with the document types shown in Figure 3.3. Compliance services can be turned on for multiple document types. Typically, you would want to map multiple sales document types from R/3 to a customs document type in GTS and multiple delivery document types from R/3 to a different customs document type.

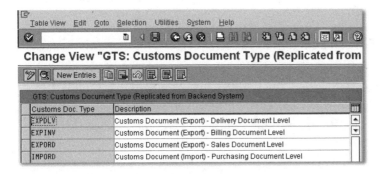

Figure 3.3 Customs Document Types in GTS

In the definition of a customs document type, you can make settings that determine how that document type behaves as you can see in Figure 3.4.

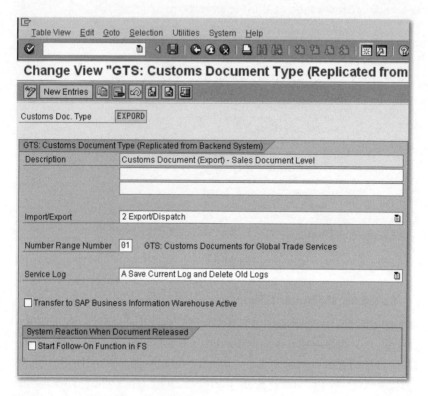

Figure 3.4 Customs Document Type Settings

The Import/Export indicator shown in Figure 3.4 determines whether the customs document type is relevant for export control or import control. This is also where you can define how the system saves the log of services performed on it.

The **Start Follow-on Function in FS** seen in Figure 3.4 is useful if you want the GTS system to kick off subsequent functions in R/3 once the document is unblocked in GTS. When you unblock the document in GTS, it writes an indicator to an R/3 work list. This work list can be processed by regularly scheduled jobs in R/3 that run the following programs:

- /SAPSLL/SD0A_OBJSSF_PROCESS_R3 for SD orders
- /SAPSLL/SD0B_OBJSSF_PROCESS_R3 for SD deliveries
- /SAPSLL/MM0A_OBJSSF_PROCESS_R3 for MM purchase orders

These programs save the sales order or delivery or purchase order, as the case may be. This save action can trigger the follow-on function if your R/3 system is configured to do so.

> **Note**
>
> The **Start Follow-on Function in FS** function is useful if your system automatically drops delivery notes for certain sales document types in R/3. In this scenario, if the sales order is blocked in GTS, the normal business process flow is interrupted. By using the **Start Follow-On Function** capability, you can trigger the save of the sales order after it has been unblocked in GTS. Because the document is not blocked in GTS, R/3 can allow the subsequent function, in this case creation of the delivery, to take place.

After defining the customs document type, you need to map it to the document types in R/3. Mapping R/3 document types to GTS customs document types is done so that when a document is transferred from R/3, it looks at this mapping to determine what customs document type it needs to create in GTS. As shown in Figure 3.5, document type **TA**, which is a standard order **OR** in R/3, is mapped to customs document type **EXPORD**. Similarly, the delivery type **LF** in R/3 is mapped to customs document type **EXPDLV** in GTS.

Mapping of customs document type can be done at a feeder system or feeder system group level. If your business scenario has multiple R/3 or other back-end systems connecting to one central GTS, you can map them at the feeder system group level.

The transfer of documents from R/3 to GTS is controlled on the R/3 side by customizing settings. There may not be a business need to transfer all document types. Transaction /SAPSLL/TLER3_B_R3 lets you turn on transfer by **Document Types**, as illustrated in Figure 3.6.

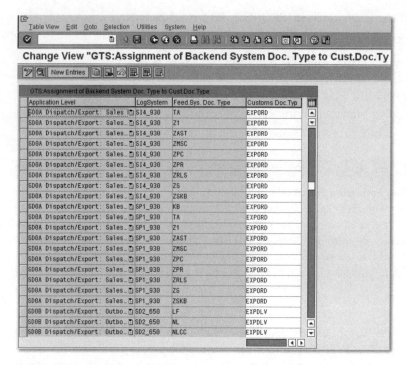

Figure 3.5 R/3 Document Type Mapping to GTS Customs Document Type

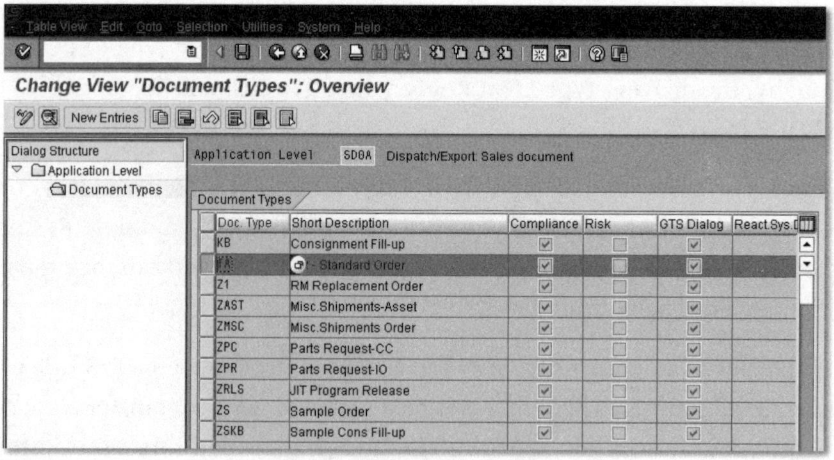

Figure 3.6 R/3 Document Type Relevant for Transfer to GTS

This is also where you determine what services these document types will consume in GTS. As shown in Figure 3.7, you can see that document type will be using Compliance Management Services in GTS. This is also where you can specify that the order-entry person working in R/3 should be able to see the results of the services performed by GTS. You can also specify the behavior of the R/3 system if the GTS system is down. In the event that GTS is down, you have one of the two options given below:

▸ Allow document to be saved but don't allow any subsequent process

▸ Subsequent process is allowed

The latter allows delivery note creation for a sales or stock transport order even though GTS is not available for the system to look up the status of the document.

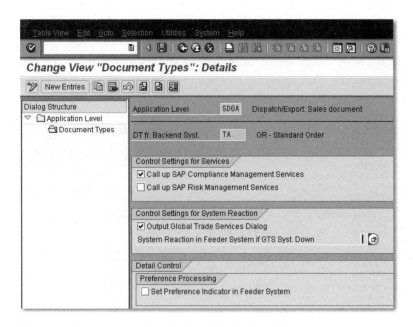

Figure 3.7 Document Type Transfer Detail Settings in R/3

3.1.2   Customs Item Category

Item categories determine the behavior of the document item in GTS, just as they do in R/3. For each service that's configured for a document type in GTS, the item category is used to make settings specific to that service. Standard GTS comes with the item categories shown in Figure 3.8.

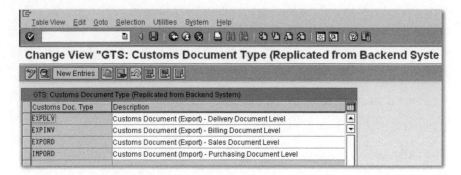

Figure 3.8 Standard Customs Item Categories in GTS

After defining customs-item categories, you need to map them to the item categories coming across on the documents from your feeder R/3 system. Figure 3.9 shows the logical system name of the back-end R/3 system, the item category that's coming over, and the customs-item category that it maps to.

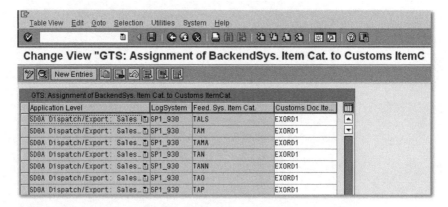

Figure 3.9 R/3 Item Category Mapped to Customs Item Category in GTS

3.1.3 Partner Functions

Partner functions determine the role of a business partner in a document. For instance, the **AG** or **Sold-to Party** function is the person or entity that enters into a sales transaction with your company, while the **WE** or the **Ship-to Party** is the person or entity that will receive the goods. GTS comes with the partner functions shown in Figure 3.10.

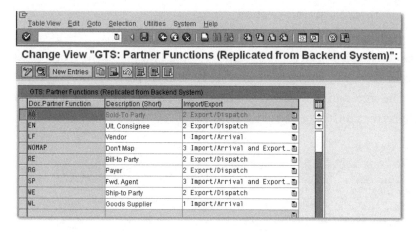

Figure 3.10 GTS Partner Functions

Partner function details determine the type of transaction that it is valid e.g., exports or imports. This is also where you specify the partner function type (see Figure 3.11). Partner function type is used by GTS to determine the validity of a partner function for certain uses. For example, the partner function of type **CUSVER Consignor/Exporter** is used for AES declarations. We talked about partner functions. Now let's talk about another concept in GTS, partner function groups.

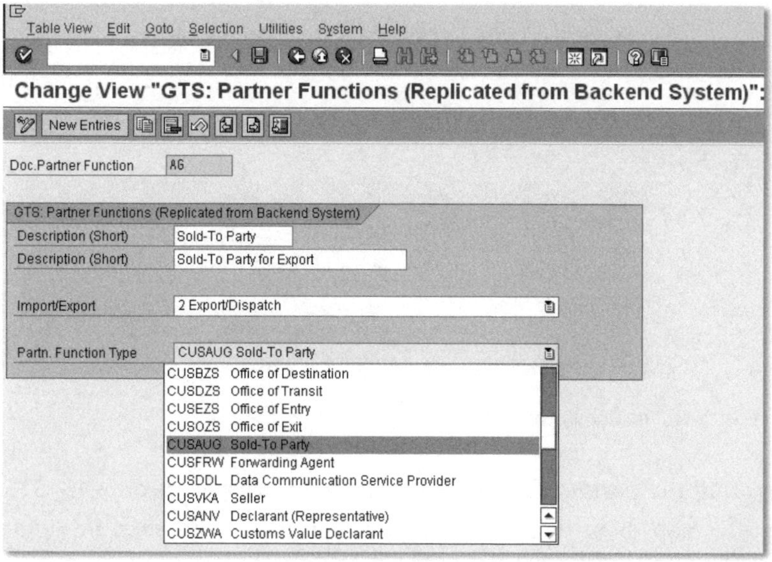

Figure 3.11 Partner Function Detail

3.1.4 Partner Function Groups

Partner function groups, as the name indicates, groups partner functions that can then be subjected to the same services in GTS. For instance, partner group **PGSPL2**, shown in Figure 3.12, has all partner functions that need to be screened against boycott lists. Figure 3.13 shows all the partner functions that constitute partner group PGSPL2.

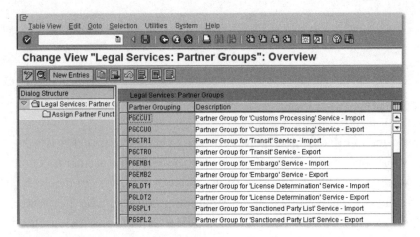

Figure 3.12 Partner Function Groups

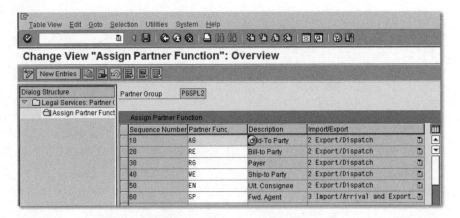

Figure 3.13 Partner Function in Group PGSPL2

After creating the partner functions and partner function groups in GTS, you need to map them to partner functions from R/3. As seen in Figure 3.14, not all partner functions are mapped in GTS.

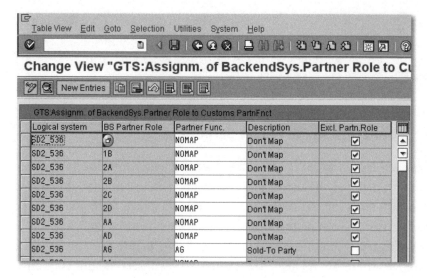

Figure 3.14 R/3 Partner Functions Mapped to GTS Partner Functions

Some R/3 partner functions that do not need to be in GTS are checked as **Excl. Partn.Role** (see Figure 3.14). These R/3 partner functions are also mapped to a special partner function on GTS that has no partner function type associated with it as seen in Figure 3.15.

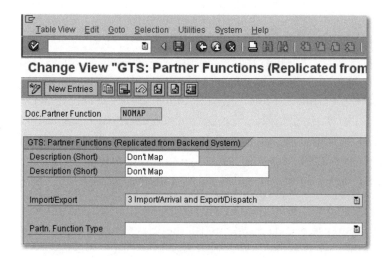

Figure 3.15 GTS Partner Function NOMAP

The **NOMAP** partner function acts as a catch all for R/3 partner functions that do not need to be transferred to GTS.

> **Note**
>
> GTS creates an error message in the back-end R/3 system if it cannot find a mapping for a partner function. It is important to map every single partner function from R/3 to some partner function in GTS.

3.2 Sanctioned Party List Screening

Sanctioned Party List (SPL) screening is a compliance function for making sure that a company has no dealings with a person or entity on the denied parties list. Government agencies expect due diligence from you to make sure that you are complying with the requirement to screen. Violation of these rules can result in severe penalties and long prison sentences. This is where GTS comes in. As discussed earlier, GTS will screen both your business partners and also documents coming from the R/3 back-end system. GTS will block these partners or documents if it determines there is a match; it then lets a person monitor these blocks to make sure they are not false positives. A false positive indicates partners or documents that GTS thinks should be blocked, but that, on closer inspection, you might decide not to block.

3.2.1 Data Providers for Sanctioned Party Lists

Sanctioned party lists are published by various government agencies. For instance in the United States, the Bureau of Export Administration within the Department of Commerce publishes the Denied Parties List. Similarly, the Department of State publishes the Designated Terrorist Organization list. In addition, if your company has global operations it needs to adhere to sanctioned lists published by the respective countries. The sanction lists are published as addendums to regulations by authorities.

In order to keep up with addition of newly sanctioned parties, a number of data providers aggregate the data and publish these lists in convenient electronic form. MK Technologies is one data provider that publishes these lists in XML formats required by GTS. Your company can subscribe to these lists and continue to receive any new additions or changes as delta files once you have uploaded the master list from MK technologies.

3.2.2 Configuring SPL Screening in GTS

In order to use GTS to screen business partners and documents from your back-end R/3 system, it needs to be configured. Configuring SPL screening in GTS involves the following:

▸ Activation of SPL screening for documents and business partners

▸ Configuring SPL check algorithm

Let us see these two configurations in more detail now.

Activation of SPL Screening for Documents and Business Partners

As for any other service in GTS, SPL screening requires a legal regulation. The definition of the legal regulation needs to use the law code **03 Prohibitions and Restrictions**, as seen in Figure 3.16.

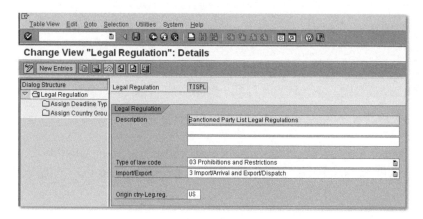

Figure 3.16 SPL Legal Regulation Definition

Steps for configuring SPL screening are available from transaction SPRO, under the SPL screening service, as shown in Figure 3.17. One of the first steps in configuring SPL screening is to indicate the business partner roles that are relevant for screening.

> **Note**
>
> All entities in GTS are defined as business partners. For instance, customers, vendors, legal units, and foreign trade organizations are all considered business partners. It's the business partner role that distinguishes their functions from each other.

Figure 3.17 Configuration Steps for SPL Screening

Add the business partner roles that you want, as shown in Figure 3.18. The partner roles for customer and vendor have been added.

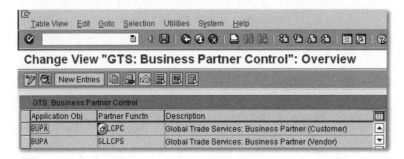

Figure 3.18 BP Role Customer and Vendor Marked Relevant for SPL Screening

In the details for the business partner role you can specify whether the partner will be screened synchronously or asynchronously (see Figure 3.19).

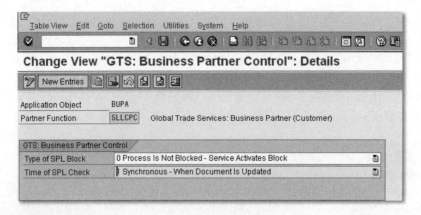

Figure 3.19 Customer SPL Screening Marked as Synchronous

Synchronous SPL screening means that the business partner is checked against SPL master data for a match as it comes across from the back-end R/3 or other system. If the system finds a match, the business partner is marked as blocked.

On the other hand, asynchronous SPL screening means that the business partner is updated in GTS but not screened. In this case, you need to run periodic screening checks at a later time on these business partners, at which time the system blocks business partners it deems a match.

Next, you need to add the customs document types for SPL screening. These are the same customs document types you defined while setting up the document structure for compliance and can be seen in Figure 3.20.

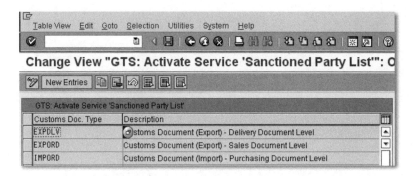

Figure 3.20 Add Customs Document Types Relevant for SPL Screening

After adding Customs document types (**Customs Doc. Type**), add customs-item categories relevant for SPL (see Figure 3.21).

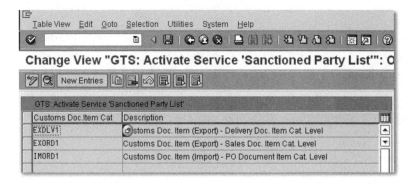

Figure 3.21 Add Customs-Item Categories Relevant for SPL

In the details of the item categories, you determine the time of the SPL check for the document. As shown in Figure 3.22, you can have a synchronous SPL check on the document partners. This means the SPL check is run as the document is updated from the back-end R/3 system to GTS. The other option is asynchronous checking. With this option, you need to schedule batch jobs to perform SPL screening of documents at a later time.

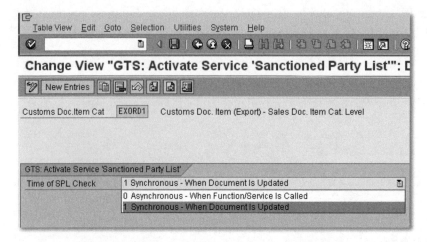

Figure 3.22 Customs Item Category Marked for Synchronous Checking

> **Note**
>
> Synchronous screening of documents does not necessarily involve checking against SPL master data to look for a match. GTS will first look at the business partners on the document. If any of them are marked as blocked, this will block the document. Only if a partner address was changed in the document will the system run a synchronous check against SPL master data to look for a match.

The final SPL activation step is at the legal regulation level. For each departure country, you need to activate the SPL legal regulation (see Figure 3.23). SPL checks can be activated for purchase orders (Import) and for sales orders and outbound delivery notes (Export). In activating SPL screening, you can include domestic business transactions or exclude them.

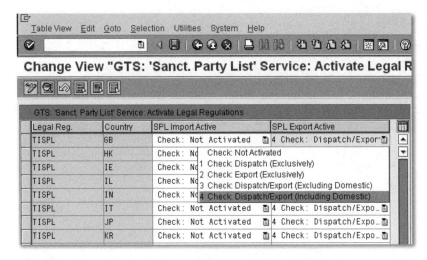

Figure 3.23 Activating SPL Legal Regulation for Departure Countries

Configuring SPL Check Algorithm

The SPL check algorithm determines what constitutes a match of the business partner with the SPL master data. The first step in configuring the SPL check algorithm is to assign a determination procedure to all active SPL legal regulations (see Figure 3.24).

Figure 3.24 Assign Determination Procedure to Active SPL Legal Regulations

Then you can define a control procedure for SPL checks (see Figure 3.25). This control procedure in turn specifies the matching algorithm.

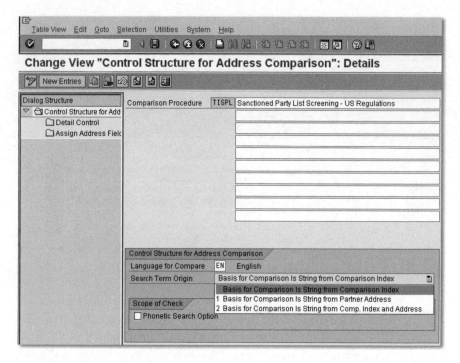

Figure 3.25 SPL Control Procedure Definition

As seen in Figure 3.25, the **Search Term Origin** setting specifies whether the system starts comparison from SPL index or partner index. SPL master data is uploaded and used to create index, which in turn is used for SPL checking. Similarly, the business partners are transferred from the backend systems and used to create another index. The **Search Term Origin** can be set so that GTS looks for a match by starting with the SPL data index. GTS also can be set to start with partner address and use it to look for a match in the SPL master data index, or to use both methods.

You can also specify a phonetic search. Phonetic search enables searches based on how a certain text sounds rather than how it is spelled. For instance, with phonetic option you can specify that Khaddafi is a replacement string for "Quaddafi." GTS will then treat the two strings as a match even though they are spelled differently. It is possible to specify complex conditions in defining phonetic search terms.

Detail Control specifies the different parts of an address that need to match. Based on these settings the system considers whether the partner address matches the SPL entry. As you can see in Figure 3.26, the Name and at least one of the categories **Country**, **Street** or **City** has to be a match for the partner address to be considered a match to the SPL entry.

Detail Control				
Search Term Origin		Check Object	Linking Operator	
C1 Keyword Generated from Country	🗎	☑	0 Logical OR (at 1🗎	▲
I1 Keyword Generated from City	🗎	☑	0 Logical OR (at …🗎	▼
N1 Keyword Generated from Name	🗎	☑	1 Logical AND	🗎
S1 Keyword Generated from Street Name	🗎	☑	0 Logical OR (at …🗎	
	🗎			🗎

Figure 3.26 SPL Match Settings

Figure 3.26 can be expressed as a mathematical Boolean logic expression in the following form: Name AND (Country OR City OR Street).

You can tweak this expression to meet the match requirements, based on your specific business scenario. Furthermore, you can specify thresholds for each component of the address. For example, for the **Name** component of the address you can specify the sensitivity in considering whether a match is made. As shown in Figure 3.27, the search term of individual words in the name have to match at least 70 %. Of the full name, at least 51 % of the words have to match.

Search Term Origin	N1 Keyword Generated from Name	🗎

Detail Control		
☑ Check Object		
Search Term Origin	Basis for Comparison Is String from Comparison Index	🗎
Linking Operator	1 Logical AND	🗎
Relational Operator	B Comparison Index and Keyword from Address Are Identical	🗎

Minimal Similarity		
Search Term	70.00	%
Original Form	51.00	%

Figure 3.27 SPL Matching Sensitivity

Example 1

1. Business partner name: Pat Wilkes

2. SPL Entry: Patrick Mckay

3. Patrick has three letters in common with Pat; hence the match is 3/3 or 100 % > 70 % threshold for search term.

4. McKay has one letter in common with Wilkes, hence the match is 1/6 or 16 % < 70 % threshold for search term.

5. Patrick Mckay has two search terms; one for each word in the name. Based on search-term settings, one of two is considered a match. That means ½ = 50 % < 51 % threshold for the original form. This business partner name is deemed to not match the SPL entry.

Example 2

1. Business partner name: Hwang Lee

2. SPL Entry: Huang Elle

3. Huang has four letters in common with Hwang, hence the match is 4/5 or 80 % > 70 % threshold for search term

4. Elle has four letters in common with Lee, hence the match is 4/4 or 100 % > 70 % threshold for search term

5. Huang Elle has two search terms; based on the search-term threshold both are considered a match. Based on original form threshold of 51 %, 2/2= 100 % is considered a match.

Further control settings specify which group of partners is screened on a document. As shown in Figure 3.28, you can specify, in the control procedure (**Control Proced.**) the partner group to screen.

Figure 3.28 Partner Group to Screen for Import/Export

Further settings in the control procedure are shown in Figure 3.29. They include the following:

► **Consider Validity**
Whether to consider validity dates of SPL master records.

► **Include Master Records Flagged for Deletion**
Ignore or consider them in finding a match.

► **Check All Origins**
Should the system compare different parts of an address or strictly compare Names with name, Street with street, etc?

► **Search Strategy**
Start with SPL entry and try to find a match with the partner address, or start with partner address and then look for a match with SPL entry.

► **Consideration of Past SPL Results**
Ignore partners that have been checked and unblocked before, or check partners every time.

► **Write Entry to Audit File**
Every time a business partner or document is screened, the system can write an audit entry of the person who screened, date, time, and comments if any. You can see this in Figure 3.30.

► **Application Buffers and/or to Cluster Tables**
The system gives you the option of storing the comparison index to application buffers and/or to cluster tables for faster screening performance, as seen in Figure 3.30.

► **Sending of Mail**
This option lets you configure sending of mail notifying of a SPL blocked business partner or document.

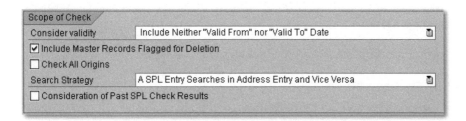

Figure 3.29 SPL Screening Comparison Procedure Settings

In addition, you can control the time of initialization of the comparison index. You can choose between the time when a new delta SPL file is uploaded and a later stage when you are re-creating indexes after the upload of a delta SPL file also seen in Figure 3.30.

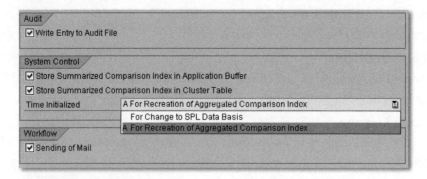

Figure 3.30 More SPL Screening Comparison Procedure Settings

> **Note**
>
> Which time-initialized option to use depends on your business process for uploading a delta SPL file. If there is a long time gap between the time you upload a delta SPL file and the time you re-create indexes, you should choose the option **A For Recreation of Aggregated Comparison Index**. However, if you have automated the entire process of uploading the delta SPL file and the subsequent recreation of indexes, choose option **For Change to SPL Data Basis**.

List Types in SPL

As we discussed at the beginning of this chapter, various governmental agencies publish denied-party lists. These lists manifest themselves in the electronic form provided by data aggregators under their own list type. In order to successfully upload the electronic lists and their contents, the list types need to be defined ahead of time in the SPL configuration in GTS (see Figure 3.31).

The definition of each list type includes the following:

▶ Letter codes for the list types e.g., **AUC**.

▶ Description with some indication of what it is and which government entity issued it. For example, MVC is merchant vessels Cuba published by Office of Foreign Assets Control (OFAC) within the U.S. Department of the Treasury.

▶ Government agency responsible for the list; it can be created as a business partner in GTS and added to the list type definition.

▶ Minimum length of index entries (see Figure 3.32) controls the length of the word that is required for it to be indexed. For instance in Figure 3.32, the length of name has to be at least two characters long to be considered for indexing and matching.

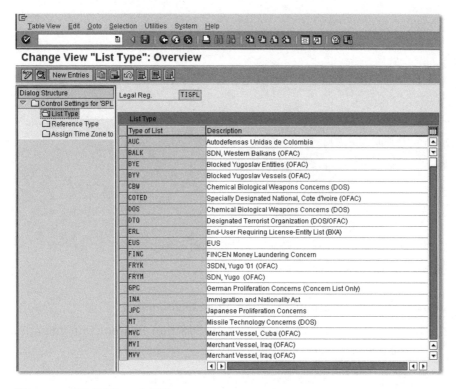

Figure 3.31 SPL List Types in GTS

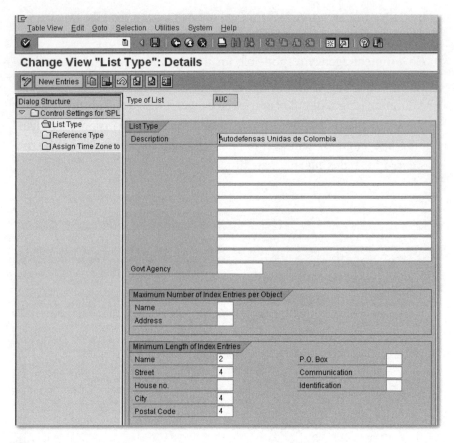

Figure 3.32 List Type Detail Settings

Monitoring SPL Screening in a Production Environment

In order to start using SPL services in a production environment, you need to do the following (also see Figure 3.33):

▶ Set up general settings that control SPL indexing

▶ Upload sanctioned party lists from data providers

▶ Index SPL data and business partners

▶ Start screening business partners and documents

▶ Monitor blocked partners and documents

▶ Use SPL screening audit trail

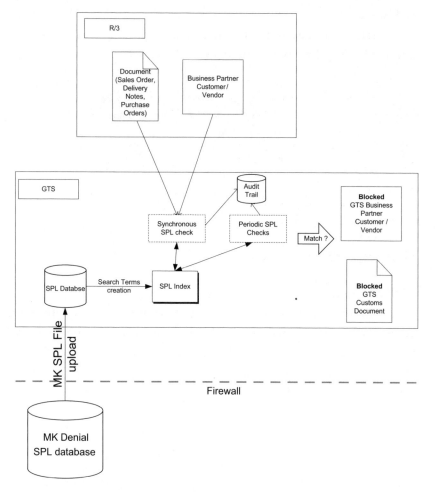

Figure 3.33 SPL Indexing and Screening

Let us look at these in detail below:

► **General Settings**

General settings for SPL provide further controls for the way SPL data records are indexed. GTS looks for a match by comparing business partner names and addresses to the index of the SPL master data rather than to the actual SPL master data. Using the index to compare optimizes the screening process for better performance as the system is using an index. These are the general settings you need to maintain in the system for SPL screening:

▶ **Delimiters**

Characters that are to be ignored while indexing SPL data are defined here and shown in Figure 3.34.

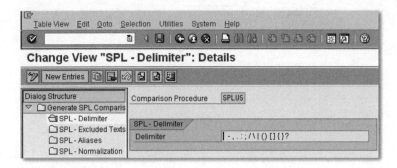

Figure 3.34 Delimiters

▶ **Excluded Text**

Words in SPL data records that are too general to be considered for comparison can be added to this list. The system ignores these words while indexing, which means they are not even part of comparison when GTS screens partners and documents. Figure 3.35 illustrates this process of exclusion.

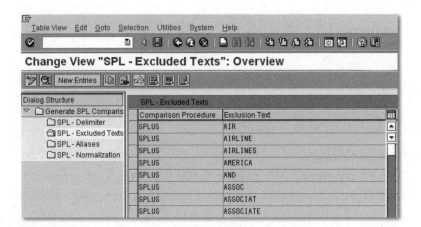

Figure 3.35 Exclusions

▶ **Aliases**

These are used to tell the system to treat two words interchangeably for comparison purposes. For example, Bob is an alias for Robert.

GTS will regard Robert Johnson and Bob Johnson as the same person (see Figure 3.36).

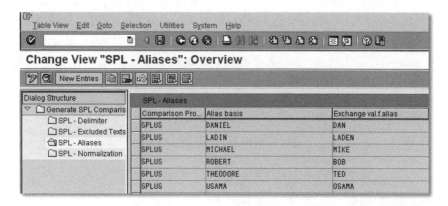

Figure 3.36 Aliases

▶ **Normalization**

This is used to replace a set of characters with another set in the index entries. This is especially relevant for German names, for instance in replacing the consecutive vowels OE with an Ö (see Figure 3.37).

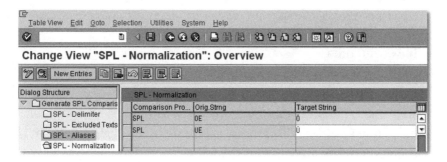

Figure 3.37 Normalization

▶ **Upload Sanctioned Party List**

Data aggregators like MK Technologies provide SPL data in XML files formatted for GTS. Typically, MK Tech publishes a master file with all the SPL entries up to a certain point in time, followed by delta files with updates to the master file, including new and changed entries.

GTS can use both extended file version and the older format, both of which are published by MK Technologies to support old and new GTS customers. The extended file leverages GTS capability to show related SPL records. In the example shown in Figure 3.38, if the system blocks business partner **ANA** because it found a SPL record **ANA**, it will show other related records with the term Albanian National Army that helps make a better determination whether it's a true match.

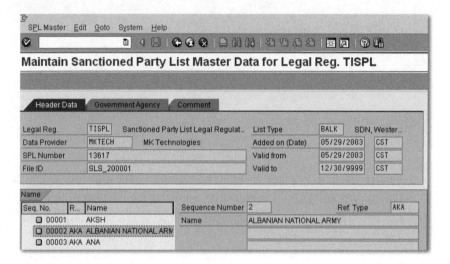

Figure 3.38 SPL Extended File

► **Index SPL Data**

After the SPL data file is uploaded, it needs to be indexed. GTS uses the index entries to compare and screen business partner names and addresses. A number of activities need to be done in sequence for SPL index to take effect. This process is repeated every time a delta SPL file is uploaded. The process works as follows:

1. Reset customizing and application buffers to remove matching algorithms from application buffers. GTS stores all data required for screening, in application buffers for faster performance.

2. Any changes made to screening don't take effect until buffers are emptied using transaction /SAPSLL/SPL_RESET Any subsequent screening reads settings from tables and writes them to buffers

3. Generate search terms for the uploaded data using transaction /SAPSLL/SPL_ST01.

4. Compress or summarize comparison index generated in the previous step, using transaction /SAPSLL/SPL_ID01. This transaction writes the aggregated comparison index of SPL data to enable faster performance.

Now you can generate a comparison index for the partner master using transaction /SAPSLL/SPL_STBP. This transaction creates an index for the business partners in your GTS system. Doing so improves system performance because the system does not have to generate an index for the partners during screening. After the initial creation of partner index, you can choose to generate this index only for new and changed partners.

After setting up the configuration for SPL screening, completing general SPL settings, loading the SPL data, and indexing it, you are ready to start screening your business partners and documents.

▶ **Screening Business Partners and Documents**
Various SPL checking scenarios are available in GTS. Depending on your business process, you can perform the ones that are relevant.

  ▶ SPL check scenario A1 and A2 check for changed business partner and document addresses respectively. As explained earlier in the chapter, SPL checking can be done synchronously or asynchronously. A1 and A2 check scenarios are for GTS customers that decide not to check synchronously. Business partners and documents are transferred from the back-end R/3 system and marked for screening. You can schedule batch jobs that screen customers and documents. This option is useful for GTS customers that have large volumes of new business partner creates and changes. Screening all those changes synchronously can raise a performance issue.

  ▶ SPL check scenario B1 and B2 are periodic checks of business partners and documents respectively. This check scenario can be used to screen all business partners against the entire SPL database in GTS. Typically, if you use synchronous checking you will not need to use this scenario on an ongoing basis. When you implement GTS, B1 and B2 check scenarios are useful for one-time screening of your business partners that were mass-transferred from an R/3 back-end system.

▶ SPL check scenarios C1 and C2 are used for screening business partners and documents for one-time customers against delta files that are uploaded on a periodic basis when they are received from the SPL data provider. C1 check works by comparing one-time business partners to new SPL master data loaded within a specific date range, as seen in Figure 3.39.

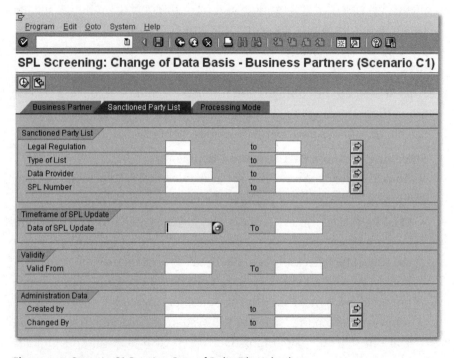

Figure 3.39 Scenario C1 Requires Date of Delta File Upload

▶ Scenario checks S1, S2, and S3 allow for the simulation of SPL checks for a specific business partner, document, or a general address.

Depending on your business need, you can use any or all of the check scenarios described. Once you start using these scenarios, you need to disposition the blocked business partners and documents that result from the checks.

▶ **Monitor Blocked Business Partners and Documents**

After all the elements are in place for SPL screening, your export-compliance personnel need to start monitoring SPL blocks on business partners and documents placed by GTS. Transactions /SAPSLL/SPL_BLBP and /SAPSLL/SPL_BLRL are used to monitor blocked partners and documents respectively. SPL simulation functions on each of these transactions show which SPL entries the system identifies as matches (see Figure 3.40).

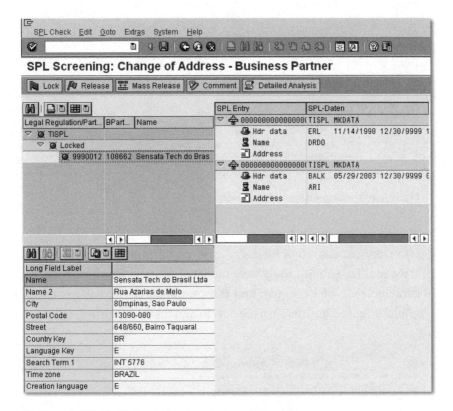

Figure 3.40 SPL Check Simulation on a Business Partner

Detailed analysis of the match shows what strings were considered a match by the system, based on the sensitivities defined in SPL configuration, as seen in Figure 3.41.

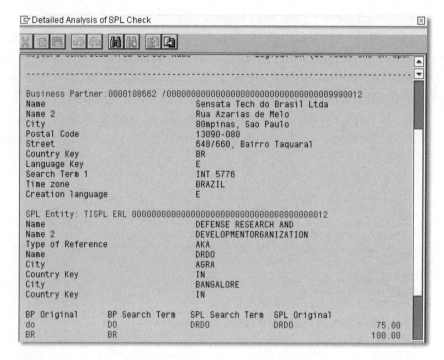

Figure 3.41 Detailed Analysis of SPL Match

► **SPL Screening Audit Trail**

GTS stores an audit trail for every business partner and document that is screened. These audit trails have the ID of the person who screened, the date and time of screening, and the comments if any were entered for unblocking the business partner or document (see Figure 3.42).

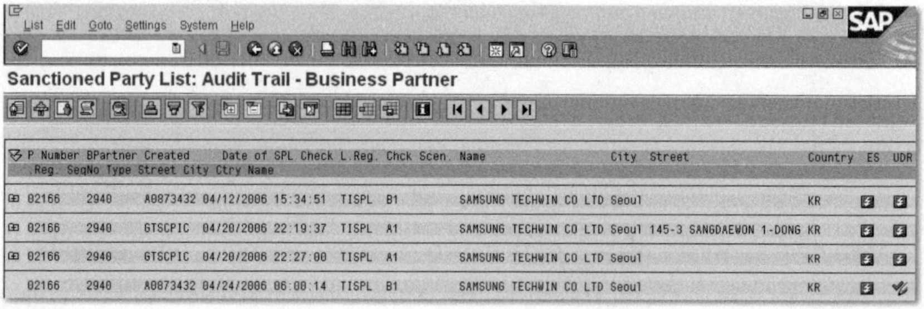

Figure 3.42 SPL Audit Trail

This concludes our discussion of the various SPL screening configuration settings, SPL check scenarios, and the activities that need to be undertaken on a daily basis so your export compliance personnel can make full use of the capabilities.

3.3 Conclusion

In this chapter, we talked about the Compliance Management module in GTS, the document structure, and how it maps to documents from R/3 back-end system. We delved into the details of SPL screening configuration and production use. This covers one of the three main compliance services in GTS.

Using GTS SPL screening services helps your company comply with one of the major requirements under the Export Administration Regulations that stipulate due diligence for a U.S.-based company to make sure it is not involved in business dealings with denied parties. Chapter 4 will take us through the remaining two compliance services: embargo check and license determination.

In Chapter 3 we started looking at the Compliance Management module in SAP Global Trade Services (GTS). We discussed the importance of compliance management to corporate business dealings around the world. We looked at the document-structure settings that are common to all the services in compliance management. Now, let us discuss the Compliance Management module from where we left off in Chapter 3. We will examine in detail the Embargo Check and License Determination services. We will also cover the configuration and use of License Determination to comply with various licensing regimes, as well as classification of products to facilitate appropriate licensing of shipments.

4 Compliance Management—Part II

4.1 Embargo Check

Embargoes are imposed by governments to prohibit trade or business ties with a particular country, mainly for political and/or military reasons. Another category of embargoes is imposed by multilateral organizations like the United Nations to prevent dealings by member countries with a particular country. GTS enables embargo checks for both business partners and documents. Embargoes can be controlled so that a global company has the capability to route trade in a way that does not violate them.

4.1.1 Configuring Embargo Check Service

To use the Embargo Check service in GTS, you need to configure and activate it. Configuring the service involves specifying customs documents type, item categories, and legal regulations relevant for Embargo Check, as you can see in Figure 4.1.

All compliance management services use the same document structure. You can decide which document types are relevant for Embargo Check, as seen in Figure 4.2.

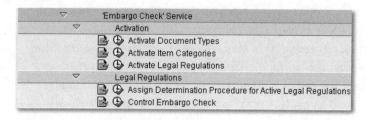

Figure 4.1 Configuring Embargo Check

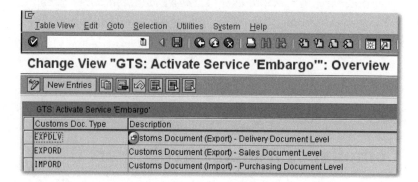

Figure 4.2 Customs Document Types Relevant for Embargo Check

Similarly, you can specify which customs item categories are relevant for Embargo Check, as seen in Figure 4.3.

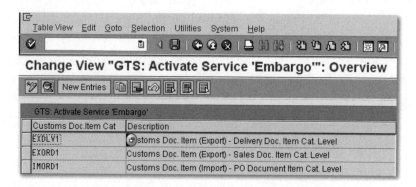

Figure 4.3 Customs Item Categories Relevant for Embargo Check

Embargo legal regulations are set up with a law code of **03**. They have to be activated for departure countries in general settings before they can be activated for Embargo Check. Legal regulation activation for Embargo Check can be done for the following (also see Figure 4.4):

- ▶ Dispatch only

- ▶ Export only

- ▶ Dispatch and export including domestic; e.g., to check for an embargoed business partner situation even if the shipping destination is within the same country

- ▶ Dispatch and export, excluding domestic

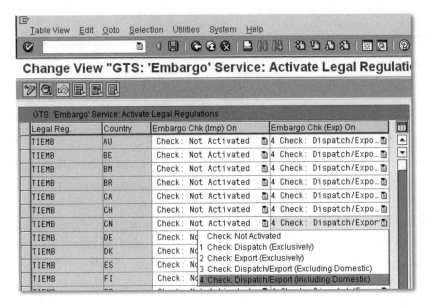

Figure 4.4 Legal Regulation Activation for Embargo Check

The final configuration step for Embargo Check is to assign a determination procedure for active legal regulations and to specify control settings for Embargo Check.

Control settings specify the partner groups that are relevant for Embargo Check for exports and imports. Only partner types that are part of the partner groups specified are checked at the document type level (see Figure 4.5).

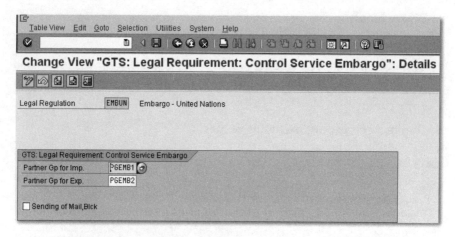

Figure 4.5 Control Settings for Embargo Check

4.1.2 Monitoring Embargo Check

Monitoring Embargo Check involves the setting up of master data and monitoring of blocked business partners and documents. Business partners are checked for embargo situation to make sure that none of the partners you do business with are in an embargoed country. Documents are checked to make sure that you are not dealing with a partner from the embargoed country and also to make sure that partner addresses changed in the document do not involve transacting business with an embargoed country.

Master Data for Embargo

GTS enables embargo checking at three levels. Depending on your business case, you can check for it at the appropriate level. These three levels are:

▶ **Country Level**
  You can specify at the country level whether or not there is an embargo, as shown in Figure 4.6.

> **Note**
>
> The absence of country information is treated as an embargo block in GTS. You need to specify both embargoed and non-embargoed countries.

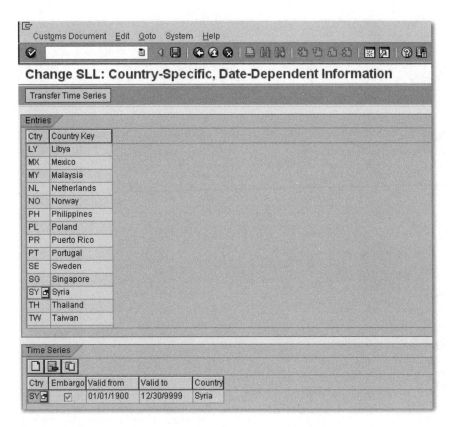

Figure 4.6 Country-Level Embargo Information

▶ **Legal Regulation and Country Level**
You can specify legal regulation and country combination for embargo. Certain countries can be embargoed under one legal regulation, while it is all right to do business with the same country under another legal regulation. This option can facilitate trade for a global company by adjusting the shipments of goods from a country that does not subscribe to the embargo of a certain destination country.

▶ **Legal Regulation and Country Pairs for Departure and Destination**
Another method offered by GTS is to specify embargo conditions for country pairs. In other words, for a given legal regulation you can specify the embargo condition from a departure country to a destination country.

> **Note**
>
> A global company can make shipments to Syria from France but not from the U.S., since the U.S. embargoes Syria. This scenario will involve a country pair of **US-SY** as blocked and setting up a country pair **FR-SY** as not blocked, as seen in Figure 4.7

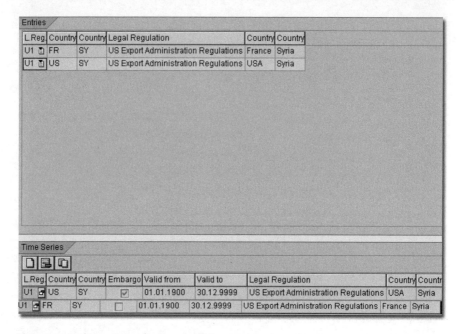

Figure 4.7 Embargo Setup for Country Pairs

Monitoring Blocked Business Partners and Documents

Business partners and documents are screened for Embargo Check as they are transferred from the back-end R/3 system. Screening of business partners and documents is done during transfer to GTS in order to block any business transaction involving embargoed countries. Transaction /SAPSLL/EMB_BLRL_EXP monitors embargo blocked documents. This transaction allows for overrides to embargo blocks and also for re-determination after setting up of embargo settings for countries. Transaction /SAPSLL/EMB_BP01 monitors business partners with embargo blocks.

We looked at the Embargo Check service and its importance in enabling the free flow of goods within an international supply chain while complying with national and United Nations embargoes. We discussed the configuration settings required to activate Embargo Check and the interaction between the back-end R/3 system and GTS with respect to business partners and documents. In Section 4.2, we will discuss the License Determination service in the Compliance Management module.

4.2   License Determination

Exports from most countries are governed by the appropriate licensing authorities of those particular countries. For instance in the U.S., the Bureau of Industry and Security in the Department of Commerce is responsible for issuing licenses for exports of controlled commodities. The reason for control may stem from regulations that are specific to that country or be dictated by multilateral arrangements to which that country subscribes. For example, the United States is a party to international arrangements that place restrictions on exports of certain types of products. Some examples are given below:

▶ **Wassenaar Arrangement**
   For the control of arms and dual use products.

▶ **Nuclear Suppliers Group**
   Focusing on products relevant to nuclear non-proliferation

▶ **Chemical Weapons Convention**
   For the control of chemical weapons and chemicals with both military and civilian use

The licensing authorities of the country publishes the list of export codes and the licensing requirements for each of those codes. All signatories to the Wassenaar Arrangement have adopted the control-lists format published by the group. This list enables classifying of products in a common language. For instance, in the U.S., the Commerce Control List specifies the export control classification number and the appropriate license requirement for that classification for a given destination country.

In the U.S., export license along with other trade requirements are governed by the Export Administration Regulations published by Bureau of Industry and Security within the Department of Commerce. For the most part, products can be exported under a license exception, which means exporters don't need to apply for a specific license to export. However, some products—as indicated by their classifications—can only be exported under a specific license that is applied for and obtained in advance of shipment.

4.2.1 License Determination Process Flow

The License Determination service in the Compliance module works on the basis of the classification of products and the rules that determine license requirements for those classifications. The steps for License Determination are:

1. Product master data is transferred from your back-end R/3 system, and once in GTS, is classified with an appropriate export control classification number (ECCN).

2. The License Determination rules are set up with license requirements for each ECCN and destination country combination.

3. License masters are created for license exceptions as determined by the country regulations. Any licenses specific to a customer or to a transaction are applied for and created in GTS after approvals from the licensing authorities.

4. When sales orders or deliveries are created in the back-end R/3 system, they come across to GTS and follow the process diagrammed in Figure 4.8 to determine an appropriate license to apply.

4.2.2 Configuring License Determination

Configuring License Determination involves a series of steps dictated by your business requirements. Each of these steps influences the behavior of the system and also the requirements the system has from the users.

License Determination shares the document structure with the SPL and Embargo Check services. One of the first steps in configuring the License Determination service is to activate the customs document types, customs document item categories, and legal regulations in the implementation guide (see Figure 4.9).

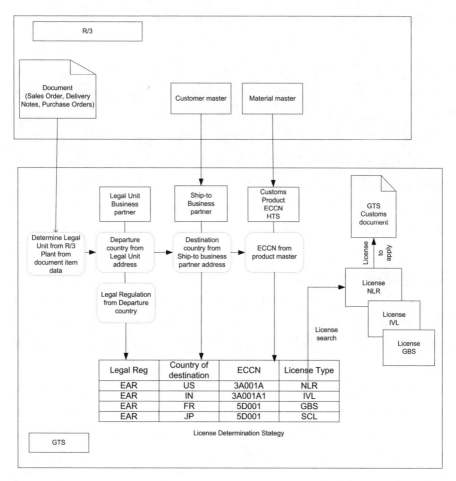

Figure 4.8 License Determination in GTS

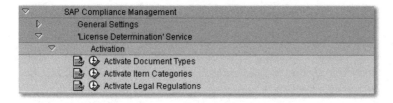

Figure 4.9 Activating License Determination Service

Activate Document Types

Activating document types involves adding customs document types that are relevant for the License Determination service (see Figure 4.10). For instance, you may not want to add quotation document types, as they don't involve shipping of products to customers.

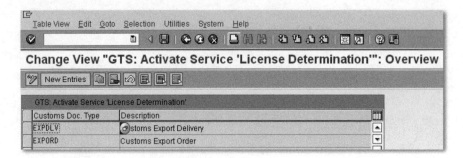

Figure 4.10 Customs Document Types Relevant for License Determination

Activate Item Categories

Activate item categories by adding customs item categories relevant for License Determination. If you will be using licenses with quantity or value limits, you can set the depreciation groups for use in the item category (see Figure 4.11).

Quantity or value limits are applicable if a government agency will only let you export a certain quantity or value of a product to a customer. For instance, the U.S. regulations require that certain products listed in the International Traffic in Arms Regulation (ITAR) only can be exported under a license approved for a fixed value of goods. In such a scenario, license applications are approved for a limited quantity or value. If you activate License Determination for both sales orders and deliveries, separate depreciation groups should be assigned to order- and delivery-item categories.

> **Note**
>
> Separate depreciation groups for sales orders and delivery items allow you to use the maximum available quantity and value for both processes, because they dip into two separate pools for the same license. This is illustrated in Figure 4.12.

If you check **Adopt Legal Control Data from Preceding Item** (see Figure 4.11), manually assigned ECCN and license are carried over from the preceding document.

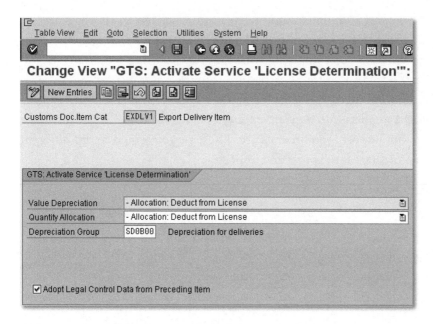

Figure 4.11 Customs Item Category Settings for License Determination

Date	Business Transaction	Quantity	Quantity Remaining
1/1/2006	License entered	100	100
1/15/2006	Sales Order 1	-50	50
1/20/2006	Delivery 1	-50	0
1/31/2006	Sales Order 2 (Blocked)	-50	?

Option 1 : Depreciation group shared by Sales orders and deliveries

Date	Business Transaction	Quantity	Quantity remaining for Sales Order depreciation group SD0A00	Quantity remaining for Delivery depreciation group SD0B00
1/1/2006	License entered	100	100	100
1/15/2006	Sales Order 1	-50	50	100
1/20/2006	Delivery 1	-50	50	50
1/31/2006	Sales Order 2	-50	0	50

Option 2 : Separate depreciation groups for Sales orders and Deliveries

Figure 4.12 Effect of Depreciation Groups on Available Quantity for a License

Activate Legal Regulations

The final activation step is to activate the License Determination legal regulation for all departure countries to which you want apply the laws embodied by a given legal regulation. For instance, a U.S.-based corporation is required to conform to U.S. export and re-export laws as laid down in the Export Administration Regulations, no matter from where it exports. Due to the extra-territorial nature of these laws, a legal regulation that is the basis for complying with the U.S. licensing requirements will typically be activated for all departure countries, not just for goods being exported from the U.S. A legal regulation can be activated for both exports from and imports into a given country (see Figure 4.13). However, since export and import requirements are different, you would set up different legal regulations for exports and imports.

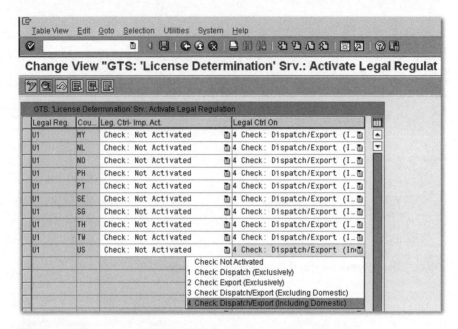

Figure 4.13 Activate Legal Regulation for Departure/Destination Countries

Numbering Scheme for Export Classification Numbers

The numbering scheme for ECCNs defines their structure. The structure of the ECCNs has to be set up and assigned to a legal regulation before ECCNs can be loaded and the customs product master is classified. ECCNs under the U.S. commerce control list are the following:

- First digit consisting of a category of the product from 0 to 9
- Second letter consisting of groups A–E
- Followed by letter combinations that specify codes for reason for control and specific product characteristics

See Figure 4.14 for the numbering scheme definition for the ECCNs as defined by the U.S. Commerce Control List

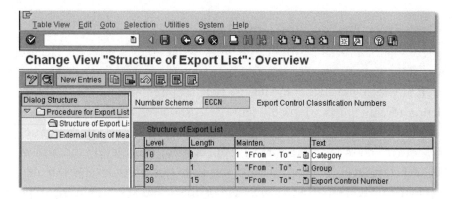

Figure 4.14 ECCN Numbering Scheme for U.S. ECCNs

Assign Numbering Scheme to Legal Regulation for License Maintenance

You can assign the numbering scheme to a legal regulation for exports and imports (see Figure 4.15). ECCNs from that numbering scheme then can be used to classify customs product master for that legal regulation and for creating licenses that require specific ECCNs.

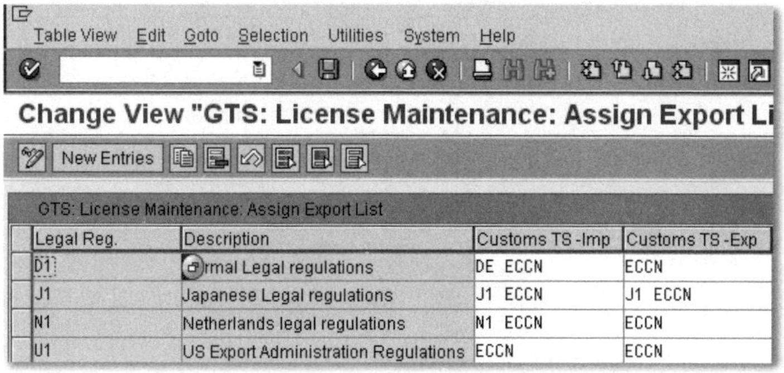

Figure 4.15 Assign ECCN Scheme to a Legal Regulation

Assign Numbering Scheme to Legal Regulation for License Determination

GTS gives you the option of using either ECCNs or ECCN groups to drive License Determination. If you choose to use ECCN groups, this configuration is optional. However, if your business scenario requires using ECCNs to determine a license, you need to assign the ECCN numbering scheme to the legal regulation, for use in maintenance of determination strategy.

Determination Procedure for License Types

Determination procedure for license types defines the basis for the License Determination strategy. In the determination procedure, you define the levels at which you can set the license type requirements for the legal regulation to which it is assigned. Figure 4.16 shows that for determination procedure **LTDE1**, license type requirements can be set at the **Country/Control class** level, **Country group/Control class** level, and also at **Control class** level. The sequence number indicates which level is searched first by GTS. Figure 4.16 also shows all possible levels at which license type requirements can be set.

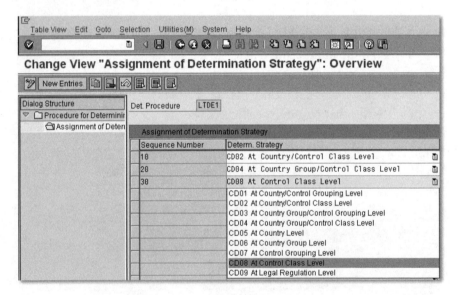

Figure 4.16 Determination Procedure for License Types

Note

Setting determination procedure at Country/Control class level means that the license type requirement will be specified by the combination of country of destination (in case of exports) and ECCN. For instance, under the U.S. regulations, ECCN# 3A991 going to country IN (India) will be shipped under a license exception NLR.

Using Country groups and Control groups (groups of ECCNs) makes it possible to reduce the number of License Determination rules because you are maintaining rules for groups of countries or ECCNs as opposed to individual countries and ECCNs.

Control Settings for License Determination

The choices you make in configuring the License Determination service are based on your business needs that influence how the service behaves.

At the legal-regulation level, you can specify how the License Determination service checks for licenses. Figure 4.17 shows the various settings, which we will also now describe.

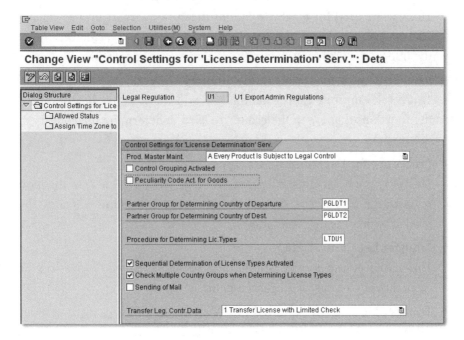

Figure 4.17 Control Settings for License Determination Service

▶ **Prod. Master Maint.**

This can be set so that all products are subject to a License Determination check. If needed, individual products can be marked as "no legal control required." Or you can set **Prod. Master Maint.** so that only selected products marked for individual control in the product master are subject to License Determination check.

- ▶ **Control Grouping Activated**

  This setting can be checked if you want to use ECCN groups to reduce License Determination rules for a legal regulation. Activating grouping also makes the ECCN group assignment possible in the customs product master.

- ▶ **Peculiarity Code Act. for Goods**

  This setting enables the assignment of a peculiarity code to the customs product master, which can then be checked in an export license during License Determination. This is relevant for German export regulations.

- ▶ **Partner Group for Determining Country of Departure**

  This can be used for legal regulations meant for import license checks. The system checks the partner types specified in that partner group on the import document to determine the country of departure.

- ▶ **Partner Groups for Determining Country of Dest.**

  This is relevant for legal regulations that will check export licenses. Partner functions that are in the group are used to determine the country of destination.

- ▶ **Procedure for Determining Lic. Types**

  This assigns a determination procedure (see Section 4.2.2.7) to the legal regulation. Assignment of the determination procedure dictates the level at which the determination rules are set.

- ▶ **Transfer Leg Contr. Data**

  This allows you to specify whether ECCNs and assigned licenses can be carried over from preceding documents.

- ▶ **Transfer License with Limited Check**

  Setting it to this will cause the system to check whether the license is expired. If it is valid, it will carry over the ECCN values and license number from the sales order to the delivery note without going through License Determination again. This is particularly useful in cases where you have to manually specify the ECCN and the license number to be used in a sales order, which can then be automatically transferred to the delivery note.

Text Determination Procedure for License Types

Text-determination procedure defines the different texts that can be maintained for a license (see Figure 4.18). The procedure is then assigned to the license types, and during license maintenance these texts can be populated. For instance, the destination control statement is required on paper documents that accompany an export shipment for a controlled product. Any customs shipment that is assigned a license with the destination control statement text has the text available for printing on generated documents.

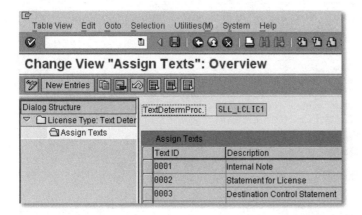

Figure 4.18 Text Determination Procedure for License Types

License Types

License type definition specifies the attributes required for a license created in GTS. The License Determination service goes through the determination rules to find the license type required by a shipment, and then tries to find a valid license of that type by matching the attributes from the document to those of the valid unexpired licenses. We'll now describe the settings involved.

> **Note**
>
> License types can be set up with roughly the same attributes as the licenses issued by the authorities.

The **Import/Export** setting in the license type (see Figure 4.19) specifies whether a license type can be used for export orders, import orders, or both.

Objects to be checked specifies the attributes of the license that must match attributes coming from the customs document in order for that license to be applied to the document.

> **Example 1**
>
> License exception "No License Required" can be set up as a license type "NLR" (see Figure 4.19). The rules for which ECCN and country of destination combination can ship under "NLR" are set up in License Determination strategy, without needing to check any other attribute on the license itself.

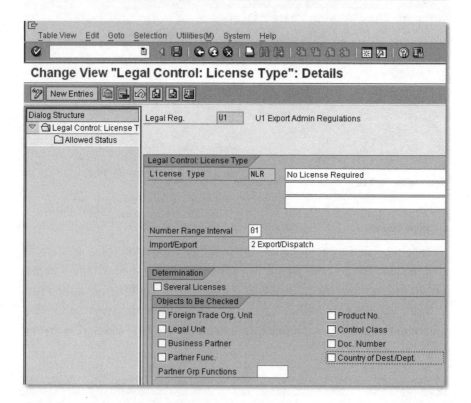

Figure 4.19 NLR License Type Definition

Individual validated licenses (IVL) are issued by the U.S. Department of Commerce for shipment to a specific customer and also for a specific quantity and value. In defining a license type to record the IVL in GTS, you would need to set the business partner as an object to be checked (see Figure 4.20). If the determination rules specify an IVL license for a customs document, the system will start looking for a valid IVL license by matching the business partner on the customs document to those on the license.

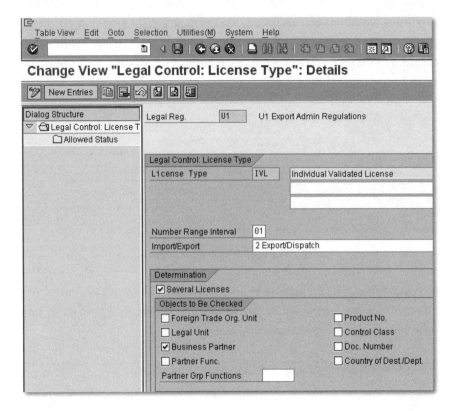

Figure 4.20 IVL License Type Definition

Some licenses are issued by the authorities for selling a certain number of units and value of a product to the customer. In those cases, you can set the license type to track the number of units and value (see Figure 4.21), so that you don't ship more than you are allowed to.

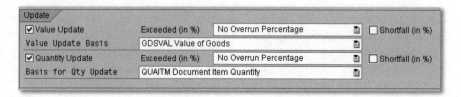

Update				
☑ Value Update	Exceeded (in %)	No Overrun Percentage	▣	☐ Shortfall (in %)
Value Update Basis	GDSVAL Value of Goods		▣	
☑ Quantity Update	Exceeded (in %)	No Overrun Percentage	▣	☐ Shortfall (in %)
Basis for Qty Update	QUAITM Document Item Quantity		▣	

Figure 4.21 Value and Quantity Tracking Settings for License Type

In conjunction with the attributes that you set for a license type, you can also control whether you can specify one or many values for that attribute. For instance, in Figure 4.22, the **Business partner** is set to have **Unlimited Number of Possible Attributes**. In maintaining the license, you can make it valid for multiple business partner numbers.

Objects That Can Be Maintained in License Master		
Foreign Trade Org. Unit	No Possible Attributes	▣
Legal Unit	No Possible Attributes	▣
Business Partner	B Unlimited Number of Possible Attributes	▣
Country of Departure/Dest.	No Possible Attributes	▣
Document Number	No Possible Attributes	▣
Product Number	No Possible Attributes	▣
Control Class	No Possible Attributes	▣

Figure 4.22 Setting for Number of Possible Attributes in a License

Additional settings in the license type definition can be used to control the use of the license for military or civilian use. As shown in Figure 4.23, this license type has the usage inspection turned on.

Military/Civilian Use and Classification			
Usage Inspection Level	2 Check at License Level		▣
Partner Usage in Partner Group	PGLDT2		
Military/Civilian Use		▣	
Classification Inspection Level	2 Check at License Level		▣
Partner Classif. in Partner Grp	PGLDT2		
☐ Missile Technology	☐ Biochemical Warfare	☐ Drugs	
☑ National Security	☐ Nuclear Nonprolif.		

Figure 4.23 Military/Civilian Usage Check

In creating a license for this license type, you can specify the usage for which this license is valid. For instance, in Figure 4.24 this license is valid only for civilian use.

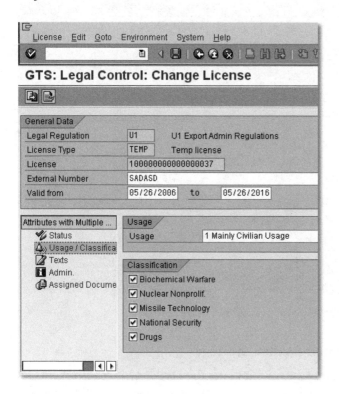

Figure 4.24 License Valid for Civilian Use Only

Depending on the classification of the business partner, this license can or cannot be used by a customs document. If the business partner is marked as being a **Mainly Military Usage** customer (see Figure 4.25), the License Determination service will deem this license to be unsuitable because it is meant for civilian use.

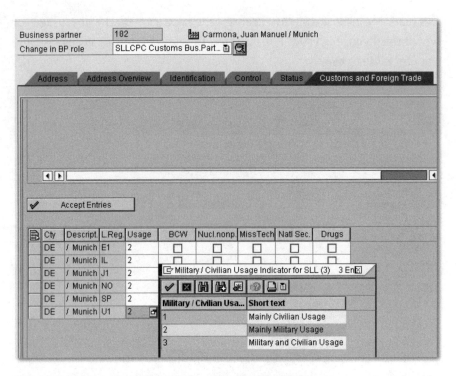

Figure 4.25 Business Partner Classified as Military Usage Customer

4.2.3 License Determination Strategy

License Determination strategy stipulates the license type requirements for any given export or import scenario. The configuration of the License Determination strategy can be set at any of the nine available levels that involve ECCN, ECCN groups, country, and country groups in different combinations (see Figure 4.16). Depending on the configuration of the determination procedure, transaction /SAPSLL/CD_MAINTAIN presents ECCN, ECCN groups, countries, and country groups for maintaining the strategy. In Figure 4.26, determination strategy is being maintained at the ECCN and country combination level. For instance, for country DE and ECCN 3A001A1B, the system will check to see if there is a valid license of type NLR available for use.

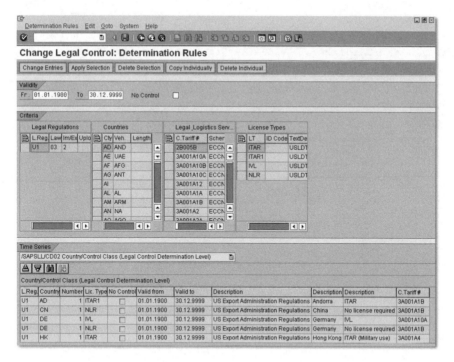

Figure 4.26 License Determination Strategy at Country/ECCN Level

Country Groups

The use of country groups in License Determination makes it possible to set license requirements for a group of countries, without having to maintain individual countries. This makes it possible to have fewer determination rules and change requirements for all countries in the group if the government regulations change. In order to use country groups in License Determination, maintain country groups as shown in Figure 4.27.

Maintain License Determination strategy using country groups as shown in Figure 4.28.

Control Groups

Control groups or ECCN groups function in much the same way as country groups do. Using Control groups, it is possible to maintain license requirements for groups of ECCNs, thus reducing the amount of determination rules and making it easier to keep up with changing regulations. Maintain Control groups using transaction /SAPSLL/CCGR as shown in Figure 4.29.

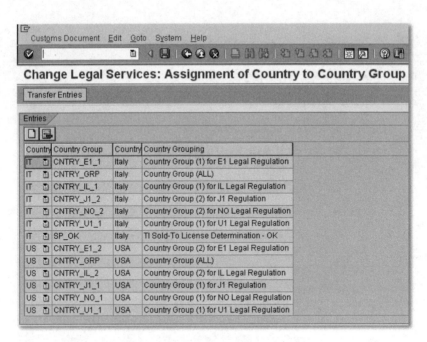

Figure 4.27 Country Assignment to Country Groups

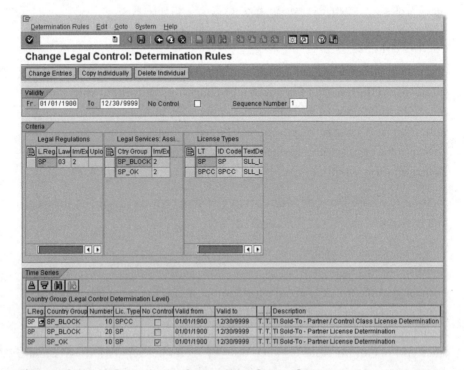

Figure 4.28 License Determination Strategy Using Country Groups

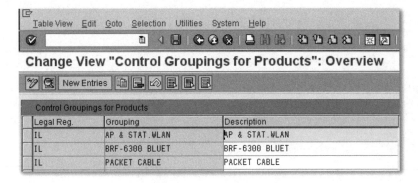

Figure 4.29 Control Groupings Maintenance

The use of Control groups for License Determination involves assignment of control group to the customs product master. The system uses Control group assigned to the product master in conjunction with the License Determination rules to look for a valid license.

4.2.4 Monitoring License Determination for Customs Documents

After configuring the License Determination service and setting the license rules, you need to set up the license exceptions and specific licenses you received from the government authorities in GTS. These licenses are a record of the authorizations from the government to ship products. When business documents are created in R/3, the GTS licenses are consumed by the customs documents. Let's explore these license options in detail.

Maintain Licenses

You need to maintain both license exceptions as well as actual licenses granted by government authorities in order to ship products in the back-end R/3 system.

Maintain licenses and their attributes using transaction /SAPSLL/LCLIC01. Configuration of the license type determines what attributes are required to be maintained in a license. For instance, in Figure 4.30, license type **NLR** requires maintenance of valid destination countries.

Figure 4.30 License Type Maintenance

Monitor Customs Documents

When sales orders and delivery notes are created in the back-end R/3 system, they are synchronously transferred to GTS. These documents are called customs documents in GTS. License Determination check is performed on these documents to make sure they are compliant with the export control laws. The system checks the attributes of the document and, based on the License Determination rules, finds and applies the appropriate valid license to the shipment. Blocked and existing document reports in GTS (transaction code /SAPSLL/BL_DOCS_EXP and /SAPSLL/CUOR04_ EXP) provide a detail of the search for a valid license and the license number that was used by GTS (See Figure 4.31 on the next page).

Maintain Legal Control Data for a Document

In certain cases you may need to maintain the ECCN, ECCN group and license number manually in a document. Transaction /SAPSLL/LCD_ CHANGE lets you assign an ECCN for each line item of a document and also a license number to use for shipping it, as seen in Figure 4.32.

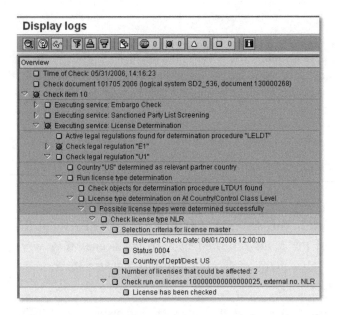

Figure 4.31 License Determination Log

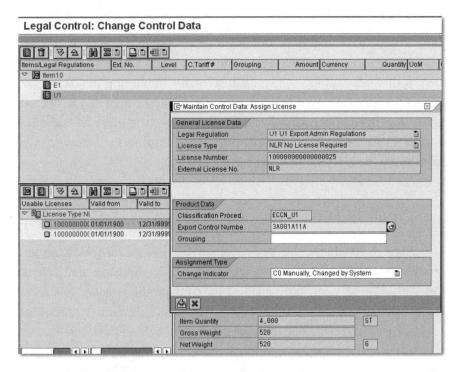

Figure 4.32 Manual Change of Legal Control Data on a Document

> **Note**
>
> You may be shipping items to a supplier that you don't know how to classify. This scenario may require further follow-up with the vendor to obtain an ECCN number for the product. Update the ECCN number in the document item, and pick a license from the available license to apply to the customs document.

Returns Process

Returns from your customers require special handling in GTS, especially if the returned items were shipped on quantity- or value-limited license. Return of items typically involves physical return of the goods and a replacement shipment. In this scenario, the return should increment the quantity and value of the items returned back to the license they were shipped on, so that subsequent replacement orders can use the original licensed quantity and value.

To make a return order increment the quantity and value back to the license, you need a different customs-item category that adds to a license, as seen in Figure 4.33.

The returns item category from the back-end system needs to be mapped to the returns customs item category in GTS. When a returns order is created in the back-end R/3 system, it increments the license in GTS, as you can see in Figure 4.34. In other words, if a customer returns 100 units of product shipped under a fixed value license, the return order adds the 100 units back to the license. The quantity added back to the license can be used to ship a replacement order for 100 units.

4.3　Conclusion

This chapter concludes the discussion of the Compliance Management module in GTS. In this chapter, we discussed the Embargo and License Determination services. We explained the configuration needed to activate these services and data setups required for using them in a production environment. We explained the legal regulations behind the License Determination and the mapping of the legal requirements in GTS. We went over the interaction between the back-end R/3 system and GTS in relation to the compliance services performed on these documents.

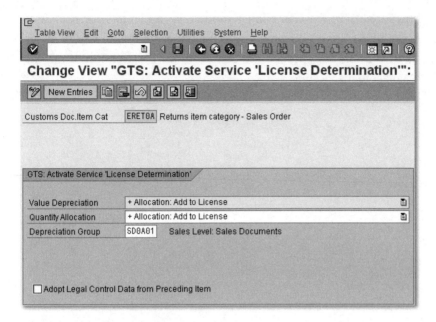

Figure 4.33 Customs Item Category for a Return Item

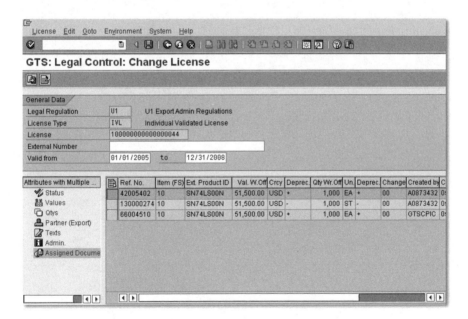

Figure 4.34 Customer Returns increment a Quantity/Value Limited License

The functionality in the Compliance module is crucial to your company's adherence to the applicable laws without hampering the flow of your supply chain. We can now proceed to Chapter 5 for a discussion of the Customs Management module.

This chapter is focused on the Customs Management module in SAP Global Trade Services (GTS). We will cover the customs communication service that enables the electronic customs declarations and transit procedures. We will discuss the trade document service and the various customs forms available for printing, customs duty calculation, and product-classification functionality that are the basis for these services.

5 Customs Management

The Customs Management module focuses on the processes involved in the flow of goods across borders through customs agencies. GTS enables the automation of these customs processes to speed up the flow of goods, thereby helping supply chains to run faster and reducing unnecessary delays and costs. A number of customs authorities worldwide have implemented IT systems that enable electronic communication of declarations and procedures and that replace a number of paper-based processes.

GTS comes certified to communicate with a number of these systems, such as the Automated Export System in the U.S. and the New Computerized Transit System in the European Union (EU). A typical export or import shipment involves a number of parties external to your company, including customs agency, freight forwarder, customs broker, or customer. The Customs Management module in GTS enables communication with each of these partners, thus facilitating the transaction smoothly. Now we need to look at the various sub-modules in GTS that facilitate the smooth movement of goods.

5.1 Product Classification

The functionality in the Product Classification sub-module forms the basis of the master data that is integral to the functioning of the other functionality in Customs Management. When outbound, shipments are declared for customs, the product being exported is identified using a common language of classification instead of company specific product name and numbers. On the inbound side, a similar classification is used to declare imports, which form the basis for assessing import duties. The Harmonized System (HS) system published by the World Customs Organization is the basis for encoding products among the 190 member countries and customs unions. HS provides a six-digit number sequence for classifying products, which is then further refined by member countries adding their specific country variation to the harmonized six digits.

HS is broken up into a two-digit chapter number, a subsequent set of two digits consisting of the heading within the chapter, and another two digits that complete the HS number, as seen in Figure 5.1.

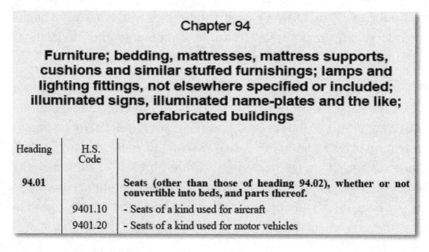

Figure 5.1 Harmonized System

In the U.S., the Harmonized Tariff Schedule (HTS) forms the basis for encoding products for import duty assessment. The HTS is published by the United States International Trade Commission. Imports into the U.S. require declaration of the HTS codes. The United States is a signatory to the

Harmonized System, so the U.S. HTS numbers are based on HS. The HS numbers have been further refined, with subheadings for more granular classification turning it into a 10-digit number, which takes its first six digits from the HS, as seen in Figure 5.2.

Heading/ Subheading	Stat. Suf-fix	Article Description
9401		Seats (other than those of heading 9402), whether or not convertible into beds, and parts thereof:
9401.10		Seats of a kind used for aircraft:
9401.10.40	00	Leather upholstered . . . .
9401.10.80	00	Other . . . .
9401.20.00		Seats of a kind used for motor vehicles . . . .
	10	Child safety seats . . . .
	90	Other . . . .

Figure 5.2 United States Harmonized Tariff Schedule

A different number is used to report exports going out of the Unites States. The Schedule B number is published by the U.S. Census Bureau and is required for declaration on exports. The declared numbers are then used for keeping statistics on foreign trade. Just like the HTS number, the Schedule B number is also based on HS, so the first six digits are the same as the HS number, while the following four digits are then adapted to U.S. export declaration needs, as seen in Figure 5.3.

Section XX – Chapter 94	
Schedule B No. and Headings	**Commodity Description**
9401	Seats (other than those of heading 9402), whether or not convertible into beds, and parts thereof:
9401.10.0000	Seats of a kind used for aircraft . . . .
9401.20.0000	Seats of a kind used for motor vehicles . . . .

Figure 5.3 Unites States Schedule B Codes

In comparing Figures 5.2 and 5.3, you can see that the HTS code is more precise because it is used for assessing duties, whereas the Schedule B numbers are used for statistical purposes.

5.1.1 Numbering Schemes

In GTS, you have to define a numbering scheme for every type of classification number that needs to be assigned to your products. For instance, in order to assign a U.S. HTS code to the product master, it needs to be defined in configuration as a numbering scheme. The structure of the numbering scheme is based on the structure of the code as defined by the issuing authority. To configure a numbering scheme for the U.S. HTS code, go to the implementation guide, transaction SPRO. Within the implementation guide, create a numbering scheme via the menu path: **SAP Customs Management · Customs Processing Service · Numbering schemes**. The numbering scheme is shown in Figure 5.4.

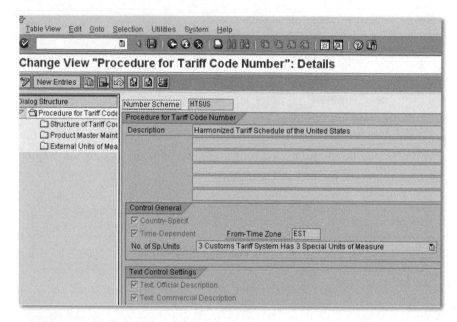

Figure 5.4 Numbering Scheme for U.S. HTS Code

In the definition of the numbering scheme, you can specify the different types of texts you can maintain for each code. Furthermore, the structure in GTS can be set up to reflect the actual structure of the coding scheme, as seen in Figure 5.5.

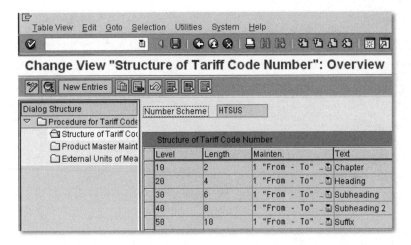

Figure 5.5 Numbering Scheme Structure for U.S. HTS Code

You can also configure external units of measure, so that when you maintain the HTS codes or upload HTS code file from external data providers, you can specify units of measure different from the ones used internally in your company.

5.1.2 Tariff/Commodity Code Maintenance

After configuring the numbering scheme, you need to populate the actual codes into the numbering scheme. GTS has partnered with data providers like FedEx trade networks in the U.S. and Bundesanzeiger Verlag in Germany. Data providers provide files for loading commodity codes and tariff codes in a GTS specific XML format file. Transaction /SAPSLL/LLNS_UPL101 and /SAPSLL/LLNS_UPL102 for loading import (tariff) codes and export (commodity) codes respectively.

You can also maintain numbers manually using transaction codes /SAPSLL/LLNS_101 and /SAPSLL/LLNS_102 for loading import (tariff) codes and export (commodity) codes respectively. See Figure 5.6 for an example of this.

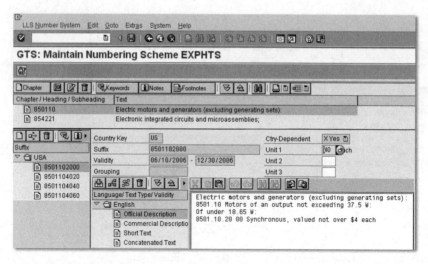

Figure 5.6 Maintenance of U.S. HTS Numbering Scheme

You can also generate help search terms for the numbering schemes using transaction /SAPSLL/LLNSCL02. The system goes through the texts for each commodity code or tariff code, as the case may be, and generates search terms. Using transaction /SAPSLL/LLNSCL01, a person classifying a product then can search for an appropriate code using keywords generated earlier, as shown in Figure 5.7.

5.1.3 Classifying Products

After configuring and assigning the numbering schemes to legal regulations and loading numbers into the numbering schemes, products can be assigned appropriate tariff or commodity codes. Using transaction /SAPSLL/PR_TRAPROC02, products can be classified for customs related codes. Figure 5.8 shows U.S. Automated Customs Environment legal regulation classifying the product with a Schedule B code for exports and an HTS code for imports.

Use transaction /SAPSLL/PR_CLASS_WB for mass classification of products in the GTS system. In this transaction, you can specify the legal regulation and the products to which you want to assign a tariff or commodity code. You can either classify products one at a time or mass-classify them with the same code, as shown in Figure 5.9.

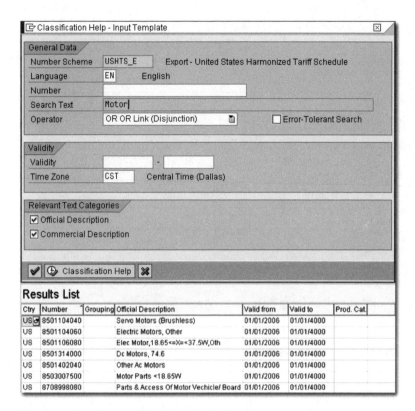

Figure 5.7 Classification Help Using Search Keywords

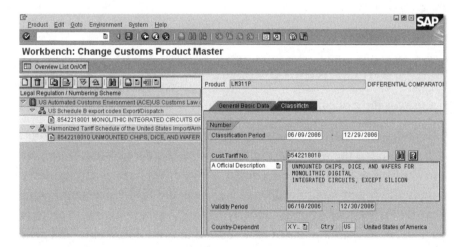

Figure 5.8 Customs Product Master Classified Schedule B and an HTS Code

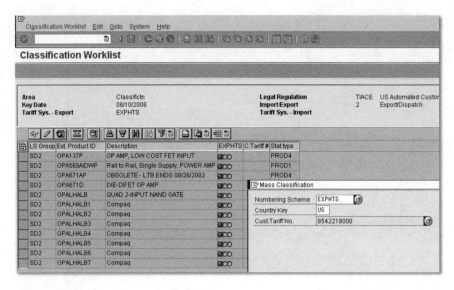

Figure 5.9 Mass Classification Using Classification Worklist

5.2 Customs Processing

The customs-processing service in GTS is devoted to trade processes that involve dealings with customs authorities in clearing shipments for your company. Customs processing encompasses three main activities, which are given below:

▶ Electronic declarations to customs authorities

▶ Printing of documents required to clear customs for both exports and imports

▶ Customs duty calculations

GTS comes enabled for declarations required by a number of customs agencies around the world. In addition, several standard customs forms are also available as a part of the delivered software. For both electronic declarations and for printing documents GTS uses the Post-Processing Framework (PPF) that is a part of the underlying NetWeaver platform. In order to send electronic declarations to customs and to print documents, you need to create a shipment document in the Customs module in GTS. The data elements from the customs shipment document are used to populate the printed documents and the electronic message. Customs shipments can either be manually created in GTS or triggered by documents from your back-end R/3 system.

5.2.1 Post-Processing Framework

Post-Processing Framework (PPF) is integral to the sending of electronic declarations and to the printing of documents. It's the technology that determines what messages need to be generated, when they need to be generated, and what method will be used to process them. GTS is delivered pre-configured with action profiles for a number of country specific scenarios, as seen in Figure 5.10.

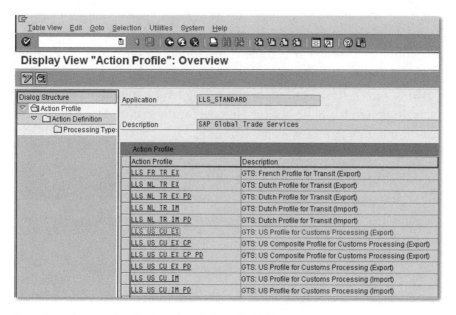

Figure 5.10 Country-Specific Scenarios Delivered with GTS

Action Profile

At the highest level in PPF is an action profile. The action profile is the interface between the PPF and the application, which in this case is a GTS customs document. Business object BUS6800 is the GTS customs document object that provides the interface with PPF.

Action Definitions

Each action profile is a collection of messages that can be processed for that profile. For instance, the profile for U.S. customs exports consists of the following messages (also shown in Figure 5.11), listed below:

- AES Outbound
- NAFTA Certificate of Origin (CF 434)
- U.S. Certificate of origin
- Shipper's Export Declaration (SED – CF 7525V)
- Shipper's Letter of Instructions

The definition of each action specifies the time frame of the action processing; e.g., immediate processing in the document, or at a later time using a selection report. Also specified in the action definition is whether the scheduling of that action is done using condition technique. Conditions specify the rules that have to be met before a particular action will be proposed in a document. For instance, you may have a condition that the customs document has to be of a certain type for the printed Shipper's Export Declaration to be processed automatically.

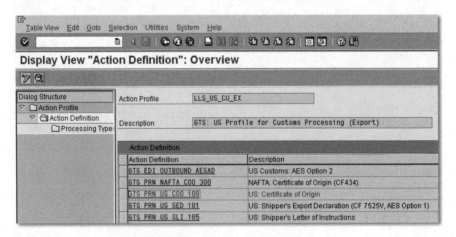

Figure 5.11 Action Definitions for U.S. Exports Action Profile

Action Processing

Action processing determines the medium to be used for processing a particular message. For instance, the printed **U.S. Shipper's Export Declara-**

tion form is processed using Smart Forms printing technology (see Figure 5.12), while AES electronic declaration is processed using **Method Call** that generates an IDOC for transmission.

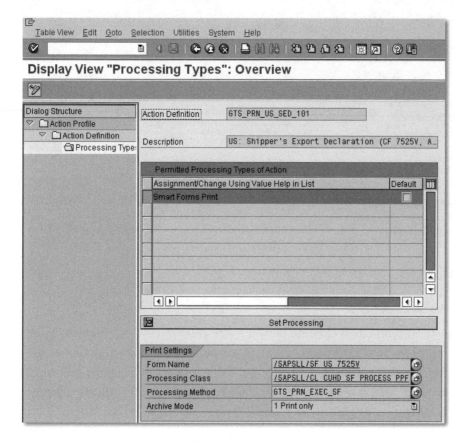

Figure 5.12 Shipper's Export Declaration Action Processing

Messages for Communication

Action definitions are further associated with a message. In the message definition, you specify the action associated with the message and in case of electronic messages also the logical message type for IDOC processing, as seen in Figure 5.13. Message determination for a proposal in a customs document is set up on the basis of the message for communication.

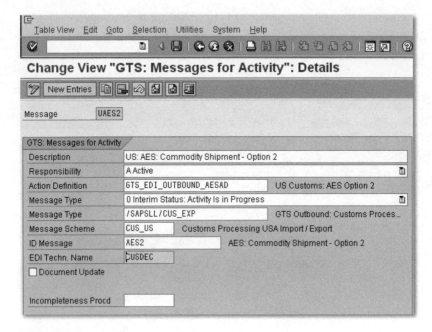

Figure 5.13 Message for Communication

Process Template

Process template is the link between PPF and the customs shipment document type in GTS. A process template is defined as a collection of messages for communication that are needed for a country or customs union. For instance, GTS ships pre-configured with country-specific process templates (see Figure 5.14) for the U.S. and a few other countries.

Process Templ.	El. Messag..	Description
CUSAU	CUS_AU	Customs Processing - AU (CLAR - ICS Export)
CUSCH	CUS_CH	Customs Processing - Switzerland (Export)
CUSDE	CUS_DE_2	Customs Processing - Germany (ATLAS SumD, Free Circulation)
CUSUS	CUS_US	Customs Processing - USA
TRSCH	CUS_CH	Transit - Switzerland (NCTS)
TRSDE	CUS_DE_2	Transit/Presentation - Germany (ATLAS NCTS, SumD)
TRSFR	CUS_FR	Transit - France (NCTS)
TRSNL	CUS_NL	Transit - Netherlands (NCTS)

Figure 5.14 Country-Specific Process Templates

Within the process template, you can further define processes to separate messages relevant for export versus those relevant for imports. This separation is done at the process level.

5.2.2 Customs Processing Service—Electronic Declarations

Most customs agencies require declarations, at the time of exports and definitely at the time of imports for payment of customs duties. Many countries have IT systems that enable electronic declarations to be made instead of paper-based processes. We will talk about the electronic declarations functionality in the customs management piece of GTS, using the U.S. Automated Export System (AES) as an example.

What is AES? AES enables the electronic filing of Shipper's Export Declarations directly to U.S. customs. All exports out of the U.S. with values of more than $ 2,500 or those requiring an export license have to be declared to U.S. customs. In order to participate in this system, your company has to be a registered self-filer with U.S. Customs. Export declarations made through AES have to be made in the formats allowed by the system, and the contents of the declarations also have to conform to the values allowed by AES. For an overview of the AES customs declarations process out of GTS see Figure 5.15.

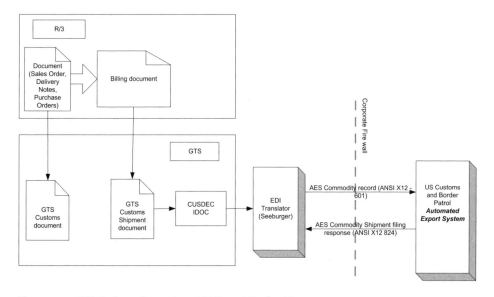

Figure 5.15 GTS Customs Processing: AES Export Declaration

Configuring Customs Processing Service: Electronic Declarations

The customs-processing service can be configured to make electronic declarations to the customs authorities. In this section we will explain concepts and settings needed in the implementation guide to activate the customs- processing service for making electronic declarations.

▶ **Customs Legal Regulation**

To configure and use electronic declarations, the first and foremost requirement is to configure a Legal Regulation for customs processing. The law code for customs processing is **01**, as seen in Figure 5.16. The next step is to activate the customs Legal Regulation for the country of departure in the case of export, or the country of destination in case of imports.

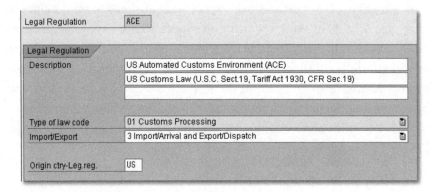

Figure 5.16 Legal Regulation for Customs Processing

▶ **Document Structure**

Customs processing in GTS is based on a shipment document which becomes the basis for calculating customs duties, printing documents, or making electronic declarations. In order to use any of the customs services, the document structure has to be configured. This involves the following actions

▶ **Customs Document Type**

A customs document type is configured to represent a document relevant for customs processing. Shipment documents transferred from back-end R/3 system and those created manually in GTS have to be mapped to a customs document type.

The settings for customs document type control include whether it is relevant for export or imports, as seen in Figure 5.17. Is access control performed at the legal-document-type level or by a combination of legal regulation and document type? This setting controls the level at which GTS looks for the messages relevant for the shipment document. The action profile relevant for this document type is the link between the customs document type and the post-processing framework. Duty calculation routine to be used with this document type is another message. In the example for AES, this routine will calculate the statistical value for declaration.

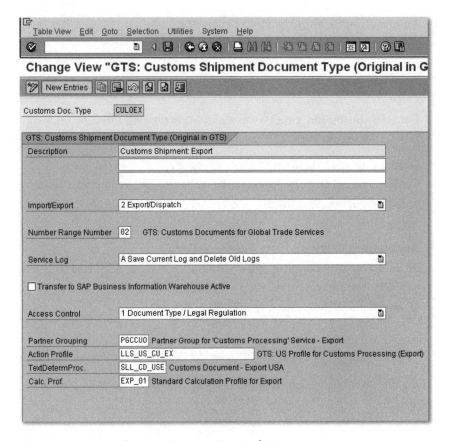

Figure 5.17 Customs Shipment Document Type Definition

► **Process Control at Document Type Legal Regulation Level**
This setting controls the printing of documents and electronic messages at the legal regulation level. This is useful if you want to use the same

customs document type for instance for exports from the U.S. as well as from Australia. In this case, you can have separate legal regulations for the two countries and assign different action profiles to each; this in turn will propose a different set documents and messages, depending on the legal regulation, even though the document type is the same.

▶ **Assign document type from feeder system**
Here you need to assign document types from the back-end R/3 system that will trigger the customs shipment document to be created.

Applic. Level	SD0C Dispatch/Export: Billing Document	

GTS: Assign Docmt Type Backend System to Custms Shipmnt Type			
Logical sy...	DType (FS)	Doc. Type	Description
SD2_536	F8	CULOEX	Pro Forma Inv f Dlv

Figure 5.18 Map R/3 Document Type to GTS Customs Document Type

For AES, outbound export shipments can be generated in GTS by the billing document from R/3, as seen in Figure 5.18.

▶ **Define Customs Document Item Category**
Customs item category controls the behavior of the customs document at the item level. Specifically, it controls customs duty calculation for the item.

▶ **Assign Item Category from Feeder System**
To complete the mapping of a document type from back-end R/3 system to a GTS customs document type, you have to map the R/3 item category to the customs item category (see Figure 5.19).

Applic. Level	SD0C Dispatch/Export: Billing Document	

GTS: Assign BSyst. Item Cat. to Customs Shipmt item Cat.			
Logical sy...	BS ItemCat	C Item Cat	Description
SD2_536	TAN	CLPOS	m for Customs Shipment
SD2_536	TANN	CLPOS	Item for Customs Shipment

Figure 5.19 R/3 Item Category Mapped to GTS Customs Items Category

After setting up the document structure and mapping it to the back-end R/3 document structure, you need to configure the customs code lists explained in the next section.

Customs Code Lists

Customs code lists are lists of allowable values that can be used in the customs shipment document and in electronic declarations. Typically, these are attributes that provide information relevant to customs agencies that are the recipients of the message. Examples of these are the mode of transport at borders for the shipment or the declaration type codes. U.S. Customs and border patrol publishes at www.cbp.gov the AES Trade Interface Requirements document, which details the allowable values that can be transmitted in the electronic AES declaration. The following configurations need to be maintained for each country scenario that you may want to enable:

► Define a procedure for custom code lists involves the grouping of code types that can be maintained for a specific country scenario. GTS- delivered configuration has customs code list procedures defined for a number of countries including U.S.

► Assigning the custom code list procedure to a legal regulation that will implement the country specific scenario. For instance, see Figure 5.20 for custom code lists that can be maintained for a a legal regulation for implementing the AES declaration.

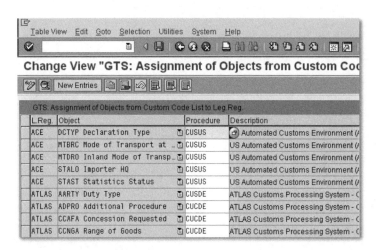

Figure 5.20 Custom Code lists Assigned to Legal Regulation for Implementing AES

▶ Maintaining code lists for legal regulation adds values allowed by the customs agency on the electronic message. For instance the U.S. Customs Service publishes the values shown in Figure 5.21 for mode of transport.

Mode of Transportation Codes

Use a Mode of Transportation Code when required in a commodity or transportation filing.

Vessel, Non-containerized	10	VE
Vessel, Containerized	11	O
Barge	12	B
Rail	20	R
Rail, Containerized	21	TT
Truck	30	J
Truck, Containerized	31	MP
Auto	32	VA
Pedestrian	33	P
Road, Other	34	ZZ
Air	40	A
Air, Containerized	41	HH
Mail	50	7
Passenger, Hand-carried	60	H
Fixed Transport Installations (Pipeline, powerhouses)		PL

Figure 5.21 U.S. Customs Allowable Values for Mode of Transportation

These values in turn need to be maintained in the customs code list for mode of transportation, as seen in Figure 5.22.

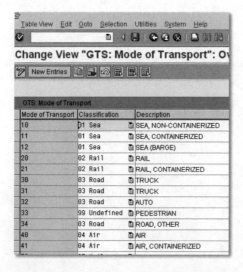

Figure 5.22 U.S. AES Mode of Transport Codes Encoded in GTS Custom Code List

Procedures for Defaulting Data

Procedures can be configured to default data into customs-shipment document fields. There are three types.

▶ Procedure for default date fields: Date fields like export date, customs value calculation date can be defaulted into the document. See Figure 5.23.

Targ.Fld	Src.Field		Lead ...	Seq. ...	Actv.
CLCTS Calculation Date	EXPTS Export Date				☑
EXPTS Export Date	$TODAY Current Date				☑

Figure 5.23 Default Dates in Customs Shipment Document

▶ Procedure for default partners: Certain partner roles may be required for the declaration or customs document that you are configuring. You can specify, for instance, partners coming from your back-end R/3 system to map to those required roles in the customs document, as seen in Figure 5.24.

Targ.Fld	Src.Field	Seq. ...	Actv.
CUSEMP	WE		☑
CUSREM	AG		☑

Figure 5.24 Default Partners in Customs Document

▶ Procedure for default fields: Any field can be configured to default to a certain value in the customs document.

After defining the procedures, they need to be assigned to a combination of legal regulation and customs document type. This step is shown in Figure 5.25

GTS: Procedure for Determining Default Data Procedure					
Legal Reg.	Doc.Type	Process	Proced. (Date)	Proced.(Partner)	Proced. (General)
ACE	CULOEX	CUSEX	0001	0001	0001

Figure 5.25 Default Data Procedure Assignment

Activating Document Type and Legal Regulation

Customs document types that were defined and mapped in creating the document structure for the Customs module need to be activated specifically for **Customs Processing Service** (see Figure 5.26). Similarly, the legal regulation configured for customs processing associated with the customs document type needs to be activated for the departure country. In our example for U.S. customs AES declarations, we configured CULOEX document type that is mapped to F8 billing type from a back-end R/3 system. Legal regulation ACE is activated for departure country U.S.

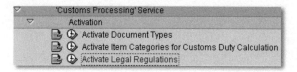

Figure 5.26 Document Type and Legal Regulation Activation

Create and Assign Numbering Schemes

We described the Product Classification sub-module in customs management earlier in the chapter. In configuring the customs-processing service, you need to create an appropriate numbering scheme for the country specific scenario and activate it by assigning it to the legal regulation for that country. In our example for U.S. AES declaration, we need to create a scheme for Schedule B numbers that are published by the U.S. census bureau. Export shipments being declared on the AES are required to specify the Schedule B number of the product being exported. Alternatively, for an import scenario we would configure a HTS scheme and assign it to an import legal regulation. To meet these requirements, we would complete the following steps.

▶ Create a numbering scheme for commodity code as shown in Figure 5.27 under customizing for transit procedure service.

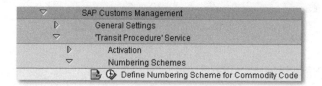

Figure 5.27 Customizing to Create Numbering Scheme for Commodity Codes

▶ Assign the numbering scheme to the customs processing legal regulation, as shown in Figure 5.28. In our example for AES, assign the numbering scheme for U.S. Schedule B numbers to the AES legal reg. Consequently, Schedule B numbers can be assigned to the customs product master, which in turn will get pulled in to a customs shipment document.

GTS: Customs Processing: Assign Commodity Codes			
L.Reg.	Import CTS	Export CTS	Description
ACE		EXPHTS	US Automated Customs Environment (ACE)

Figure 5.28 Assign Numbering Scheme for U.S. Schedule B Numbers to Customs Legal Regulation for AES

After assigning the numbering scheme for the purpose of maintaining customs classifications for a product, you need to configure the legal regulation that will implement the Customs Processing Service, as explained in the next section.

Configure Customs Legal Regulation

Configuring the legal regulation involves making legal-regulation-specific settings for customs processing, as seen in Figure 5.29. This includes the following:

▶ Assigning a determination procedure for active legal regulations

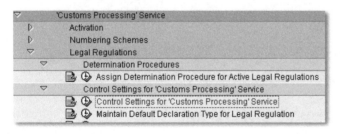

Figure 5.29 Customizing for Customs Processing Legal Regulation

▶ Control settings for customs processing service by assigning a process template to the legal regulation. This is the link between PPF and the legal regulation. Messages defined as part of the process template are relevant for declaration or printing under the legal regulation. In our example for AES, we have assigned process template "CUSUS" to legal regulation ACE (See Figure 5.30). Message UAES2 is part of this process template.

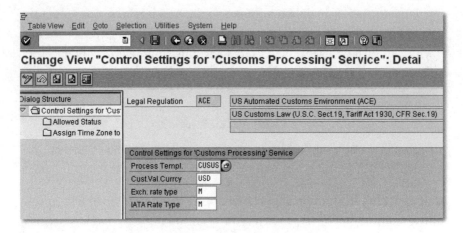

Figure 5.30 Assign Process Template to Legal Regulation

► Maintain default declaration type for legal regulation by assigning a default declaration to the legal regulation. If the customs shipment document is generated by back-end R/3 system billing document, this default declaration is made. In our example, we want this legal regulation to generate the AES declaration type "RZ." See Figure 5.31.

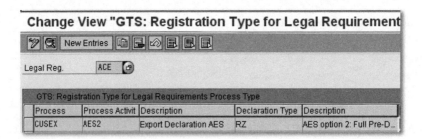

Figure 5.31 Default Declaration for Legal Regulation

This concludes the configuration that needs to be done for customs processing service in GTS. In the next section, we will explain the configuration that needs to be made in the back-end R/3 system to enable electronic declarations from GTS.

Configuration of Back-End R/3 System

For outbound logistics, a billing document from the back-end R/3 system typically would be the basis for making any kind of export declaration to the customs authorities. You can configure R/3 document transfer so that the billing document gets transferred to GTS to generate a customs shipment document and transmit electronic declaration.

▶ To turn on billing document transfer from R/3, use transaction /SAPSLL/TLER3_B_R3 to configure transfer of the relevant billing type (see Figure 5.32). Add the billing type for transfer under application level SD0C.

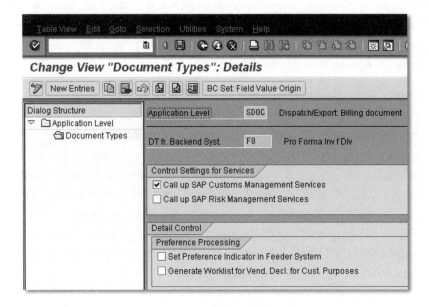

Figure 5.32 Billing Document Transfer From R/3 to GTS

▶ Specify GTS service to call, and the default declaration to make in the R/3 user exit EXIT_SAPLSLL_LEG_CDPIR3_002. See the following sample code. In our example for AES, the service to call is customs service **LECCUS** and the default declaration is **RZ**.

```
*&---------------------------------------------*
*&Include ZXSLLLEGCDPIR3U02 *
*&---------------------------------------------*
IF IV_BUSINESS_OBJECT = 'VBRK'.
 CS_API6800-HEADER-CSD-SRVLL = 'LECCUS'.
 CS_API6800-HEADER-CSD-DCTYP = 'RZ'.
ENDIF.
```

This concludes the configuration needed to generate an electronic declaration from the Customs module. In the next section, we will talk about the master data setups needed to make electronic declarations using the customs processing service. Now let's proceed to how to set up master data for electronic declarations.

Master Data for Electronic Declarations

Enabling electronic declarations from customs shipment documents also requires setting the up of master data like customs office numbers that you want to send declarations to. In addition EDI settings are required to transmit the GTS generated declaration IDOCs.

▶ **Trader Identification Number**

Maintain a trader identification number for foreign trade organizations assigned to your company by the relevant customs authority. This number is used in identifying your company to customs authorities on the electronic message. U.S. customs issues a U.S. Principle Party in Interest number (USPPI number) to all self-filers, and this number needs to be sent on the AES declaration. When creating a customs shipment, the foreign trade organization is defaulted as the consignor and the USPPI number for the foreign trade organization can be assigned in the master data for customs, as seen in Figure 5.33.

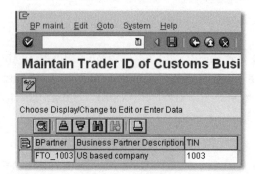

Figure 5.33 Assign TIN to Foreign Trade Organization

▶ **Customs Offices**

You need to maintain customs offices as master data for the proper functioning of the electronic declaration. These customs offices serve two purposes. First, they are used on customs shipment documents to indicate the customs office of issue and placement. Second, they are the link between customs declaration generated from the shipment document and the EDI settings that route it to the right recipient, in this case the customs office of issue.

Follow the steps below to create the customs office as a business partner to which you can send an electronic customs declaration:

1. Create a business partner in the role of customs office SLLCOF, as seen in Figure 5.34.

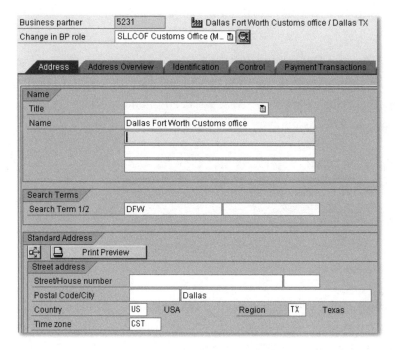

Figure 5.34 Customs Office Business Partner

2. Assign a customs office number to the business partner, as seen in Figure 5.35. This is the external identification number of a customs office given by the customs agency. For instance for AES, U.S. Customs publishes the codes in its AESTIR (AES Trade interface requirements) documents. You can also create customs offices using an upload file provided by a third-party data provider.

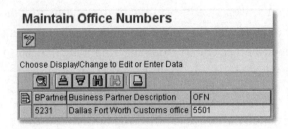

Figure 5.35 Assign Customs Office Number to Customs-Office Business Partner

3. After creating the customs office as a business partner, you need to set up message-determination parameters to generate messages from the customs documents, as explained in the next section.

5.2.3 Message Determination

Message determination is used by PPF to propose messages in customs documents. In our example for AES, we need to add message UAES2 created earlier in PPF customizing (see Figure 5.36).

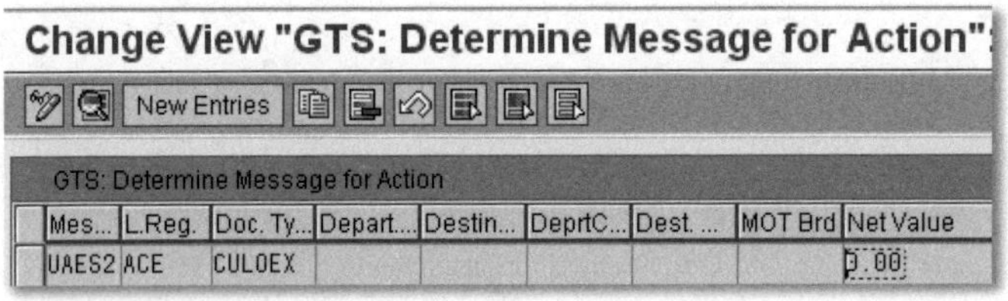

Figure 5.36 Message Determination

After setting up the master data needed for making electronic declarations using the customs processing service, you need to set up the EDI settings needed to process the electronic message generated by the Customs module. This is explained further in the next sections.

EDI Settings for Transmitting Electronic Declarations

Customs processing service uses the EDI infrastructure that's part of the underlying Basis Web application server. In order to transmit these electronic messages to the receiving customs authorities, you need to make the EDI setups explained in this section.

▶ **Partner Profile**

Partner profile is an important element of R/3 EDI communications that specifies the communication port and message types for inbound and outbound processing for a given scenario. In order to send electronic messages to customs authorities, you need to set up a partner profile for the customs office with which you are communicating. In our example for AES, you need to set up a partner profile for the customs office of issue on your shipment document and specify the outbound message type /SAPSLL/CUS_EXP and an inbound message type /SAPSLL/TRS_INBOUND for filing response message back from customs (see Figure 5.37).

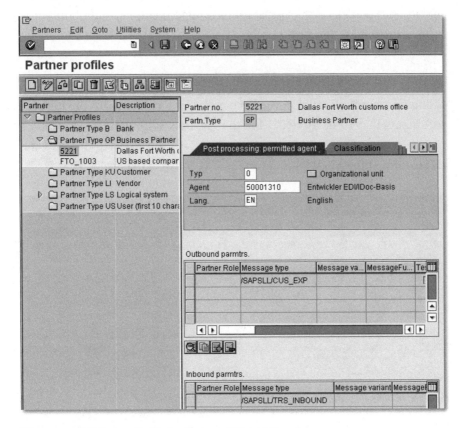

Figure 5.37 EDI Partner Profile for Customs Office of Departure

▶ **Port and RFC Definition**

In partner-profile definition, you need to specify the port to be used for outbound and inbound communication from GTS. In the definition of the port, you specify the method of communication; e.g., whether it is by file or by RFC calls to the external system. If you are using Seeburger's Business Integration Translator for converting the GTS IDOC formats to ANSI X12 601 message, you need to specify the RFC destination of the call to Seeburger software and then associate the outbound port definition with RFC destination.

This concludes the master data and EDI setups needed for sending electronic declarations to customs. You can now create customs shipment documents and send electronic declarations for goods shipped out of the country, as explained in the next section.

Creating and Monitoring Electronic Declarations

Billing documents created in the back-end R/3 documents are the logistics documents that form the basis for the customs shipment in GTS. Billing documents (see Figure 5.38) are synchronously transferred to GTS and create customs shipment document in GTS, as shown in Figure 5.39.

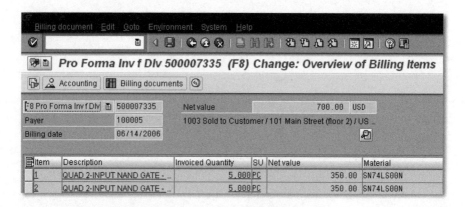

Figure 5.38 Billing Document in R/3

GTS customs shipment goes through a set of consistency checks to make sure all the required data to be transmitted on the electronic message is present and maintained in the document. You can run a manual check prior to sending the message and see the problems to be fixed (see Figure 5.40).

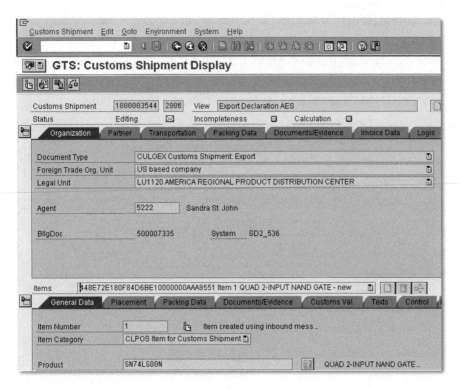

Figure 5.39 Customs Shipment Document in GTS

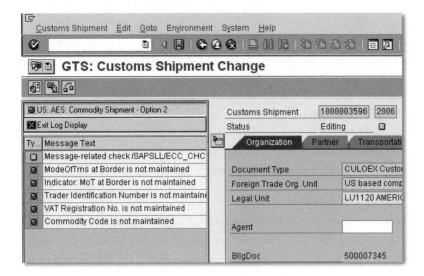

Figure 5.40 Consistency Check Results for AES Message

The **Communication** tab on the shipment document shows messages for printing as well as electronic declarations. Depending on the process template assigned to the document type and legal regulation and message determination setup, the customs shipment document automatically proposes messages. Figure 5.41 shows AES message in sent status.

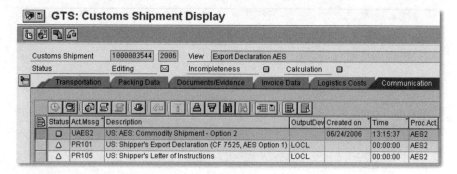

GTS: Customs Shipment Display

| Customs Shipment | 1000003544 | 2006 | View | Export Declaration AES |
| Status | Editing | | Incompleteness | Calculation |

Transportation | Packing Data | Documents/Evidence | Invoice Data | Logistics Costs | Communication

Status	Act.Mssg	Description	OutputDev	Created on	Time	Proc.Act.
	UAES2	US: AES: Commodity Shipment - Option 2		06/24/2006	13:15:37	AES2
	PR101	US: Shipper's Export Declaration (CF 7525, AES Option 1)	LOCL		00:00:00	AES2
	PR105	US: Shipper's Letter of Instructions	LOCL		00:00:00	AES2

Figure 5.41 Customs Shipment Communication Tab

Customs Processing Service: Document Printing

Customs agencies around the world mandate that information required by them to process a shipment is provided on specific forms. These forms have to accompany the shipments in order to clear customs both on the inbound as well as the outbound side. GTS Customs module provides a robust document-printing solution that includes standard customs forms of various countries delivered with the solution and new forms continually being added in newer releases of GTS.

Document printing in GTS is powered by PPF technology as already described in Section 5.2.1. GTS comes pre-configured with country-specific action profiles that group together the customs forms of that country that are available for printing in the system, as can be seen in Figure 5.42.

▶ **Configuring Document Printing**

Configuring document printing involves configuring the PPF. After configuring the messages for communication and adding them to a country-specific process template as shown in Section 5.2.1, the following activities need to be completed specifically for printed documents.

GTS: US Profile for Customs Processing (Export)				
OK	Action Definition	No.	ProcessTyp	
☐	US Customs: AES Option 2	1	Method call	
☐	NAFTA: Certificate of Origin (CF434)	1	Print	
☐	US: Certificate of Origin	1	Print	
☐	US: Export Packing List	1	Print	
☐	US: Shipper's Export Declaration (CF 7525V, AES Option 1)	1	Print	
☐	US: Shipper's Letter of Instructions	1	Print	

Figure 5.42 U.S. Customs Forms Available for Printing in GTS

► **Control Parameters for Foreign Trade Documents**

In this activity, you can specify the item description that is printed on the form. For example, you may choose to print either the product description or the description of the commodity code. You also can choose to combine items with the same commodity codes into one item on the forms. Figure 5.43 provides an example: the printed U.S. Shipper's Export Declaration combining items.

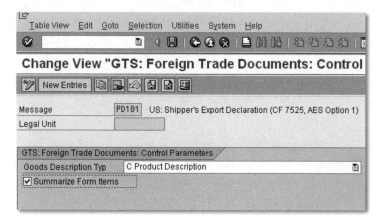

Figure 5.43 Print Control for Foreign Trade Documents

► **Configuring the Customs Document Type**

This associates an action profile with the document type or combination of document type and legal regulation. All the foreign trade documents that are part of the action profile are then available for printing from the customs shipment document (this was shown earlier in Figure 5.17). Because printing of foreign trade documents is done from the customs shipment document, it shares the configuration with other features of the Customs Processing Service.

▶ **Message and Printer Determination for Foreign Trade Documents**
Message determination is a required setup for a foreign trade document to be submitted automatically for printing in the customs shipment document. See Figure 5.44 as an example.

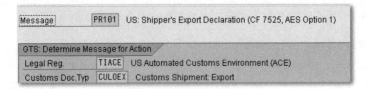

Figure 5.44 Message Determination for Foreign Trade Document

Printer-determination setup is used by the system to determine the default printer to route a particular document for printing. As shown in Figure 5.45, you can route the document for printing to a specific printer, depending on the combination of **Legal Unit** (Plant) and the **User** creating the customs shipment.

Figure 5.45 Printer Determination

▶ **Printing Foreign Trade Documents**
Printing of foreign trade documents is done from the customs shipment documents, which can either be manually created in GTS or triggered by the automatic transfer billing document in case of exports from the back-end R/3 system. Depending on the configuration and determination setups, relevant foreign trade documents are proposed for printing in the Customs Shipment Document Communication tab (see Figure 5.46).

Figure 5.46 Foreign Trade Documents Submitted for Printing

Documents can be set up to print automatically when a customs shipment document is created or at a later time. This change can be made in PPF in the action definition as shown in Figure 5.47.

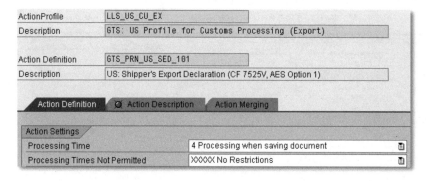

Figure 5.47 Print Foreign Trade Document Immediately

You can print-preview the document in the customs shipment to make sure all the information on the document is correct before printing (see Figure 5.48).

GTS uses Smart Forms and Adobe PDF for printing forms. Adobe PDF technology is the latest printing technology available in SAP applications; any new forms in later releases of GTS will be developed using Adobe. However, for a list of standard forms available for printing in GTS you need to go to two different transactions. These are:

▶ Use transaction SMARTFORMS for a list of forms developed by SAP using proprietary Smart Forms technology (see Figure 5.49).

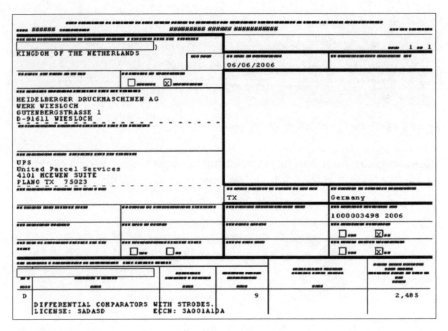

Figure 5.48 Foreign Trade Document Print Preview

Name	Description	Smart Form type
/SAPSLL/SF_CH_801A	Declaration List	Standard Form
/SAPSLL/SF_CH_802ANV	CH: Renewal Coupon	Standard Form
/SAPSLL/SF_CH_802AZV	Export List	Standard Form
/SAPSLL/SF_DE_CTAX	Import Duty Notice (DE)	Standard Form
/SAPSLL/SF_DE_CUSTST	... Internal Test - Storage	Standard Form
/SAPSLL/SF_EU_ATR	Movement Certificate A.TR.1	Standard Form
/SAPSLL/SF_EU_COO	EC Certificate of Origin	Standard Form
/SAPSLL/SF_EU_EUR1	EUR 1 Certificate of Origin	Standard Form
/SAPSLL/SF_EU_INF4	Information Sheet INF4	Standard Form
/SAPSLL/SF_EU_SAD	SAD EX/EU/COM	Standard Form
/SAPSLL/SF_EU_SAD_LL	SAD T1/T2 + Loading List	Standard Form
/SAPSLL/SF_EU_T5	Control Document T5	Standard Form
/SAPSLL/SF_EU_UNLOP_NCTS	NCTS Unloading Permission	Standard Form
/SAPSLL/SF_EU_UNLPR_NCTS	NCTS Unloading Rejection	Standard Form
/SAPSLL/SF_EU_VD_1	SF: LTVD Form Name	Standard Form
/SAPSLL/SF_GL_EPL	Export Packing List	Standard Form
/SAPSLL/SF_NAFTA_CA_COO	NAFTA Cert. of Origin (Canada)	Standard Form
/SAPSLL/SF_NAFTA_COO	NAFTA Certificate of Origin	Standard Form
/SAPSLL/SF_NAFTA_COO_SOLICITN	NAFTA Long-Term Vend.Decl.Req.	Standard Form
/SAPSLL/SF_NAFTA_MX_COO	NAFTA Cert. of Origin (Mexico)	Standard Form
/SAPSLL/SF_TNS	Tariff Number Data Sheet	Standard Form
/SAPSLL/SF_US_7525V	Shipper's Export Declaration	Standard Form
/SAPSLL/SF_US_CF3461	CF 3461 Immediate Entry	Standard Form
/SAPSLL/SF_US_CF7501	CF 7501 Entry Summary	Standard Form
/SAPSLL/SF_US_CF7533	CF 7533 Inward Cargo Manifest	Standard Form
/SAPSLL/SF_US_COO	U.S. Certificate of Origin	Standard Form
/SAPSLL/SF_US_SLI	Shipper's Letter of Instr.	Standard Form

Figure 5.49 Standard Forms in Smart Forms Technology

▸ Go to Transaction SFP for a list of forms developed by SAP in Adobe technology (see Figure 5.50).

Name	Description	Stat...
/SAPSLL/PF_CH_801A	Declaration List	Active
/SAPSLL/PF_CH_802ANV	Renewal Coupon	Active
/SAPSLL/PF_CH_802AZV	Export List	Active
/SAPSLL/PF_DE_CTAX	Import Duty Notice (DE)	Active
/SAPSLL/PF_EU_ATR	Movement Certificate A.TR.1	Active
/SAPSLL/PF_EU_COO	EC Certificate of Origin	Active
/SAPSLL/PF_EU_EUR1	EUR 1 Certificate of Origin	Active
/SAPSLL/PF_EU_INF4	Information Sheet INF4	Active
/SAPSLL/PF_EU_SAD	SAD EX/EU/COM	Active
/SAPSLL/PF_EU_SAD2	Single Administrative Document EX/EU/COM with Form Layout	Active
/SAPSLL/PF_EU_SAD_LL	SAD T1/T2 + Loading List	Active
/SAPSLL/PF_EU_T5	Control Document T5	Active
/SAPSLL/PF_EU_UNLOP_NCTS	NCTS Unloading Permission	Active
/SAPSLL/PF_EU_UNLPR_NCTS	NCTS Unloading Rejection	Active
/SAPSLL/PF_EU_VD_1	SF: LTVD Form Name	Active
/SAPSLL/PF_GL_EPL	Export Packing List	Active
/SAPSLL/PF_NAFTA_COO	NAFTA Certificate of Origin	Active
/SAPSLL/PF_US_7525V	Shipper's Export Declaration	Active
/SAPSLL/PF_US_CF3461	CF 3461 Immediate Entry	Active
/SAPSLL/PF_US_CF7501	CF 7501 Entry Summary	Active
/SAPSLL/PF_US_CF7533	CF 7533 Inward Cargo Manifest	Active
/SAPSLL/PF_US_COO	U.S. Certificate of Origin	Active
/SAPSLL/PF_US_SLI	Shipper's Letter of Instr.	Active

Figure 5.50 Standard Forms in Adobe Technology

This concludes the discussion of the Document Print Service in GTS. We looked at the configuration needed to print documents, the list of available standard customs documents, and the Smart Forms and Adobe print technologies used to generate those documents. Now we can go on to discuss the customs duty calculation functionality in GTS.

Customs Processing Service: Customs Duty Calculation

GTS provides comprehensive functionality to calculate customs duty in the customs shipment document. Accurate customs duty calculation is based on customs value calculation to which duty rates can be applied. See Figure 5.51 for a typical procedure for calculating customs duty payable.

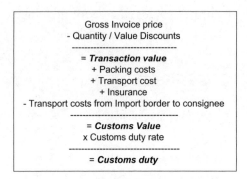

```
            Gross Invoice price
        - Quantity / Value Discounts
       ------------------------------------
            = Transaction value
               + Packing costs
               + Transport cost
                  + Insurance
   - Transport costs from Import border to consignee
       ------------------------------------
               = Customs Value
             x Customs duty rate
       ------------------------------------
               = Customs duty
```

Figure 5.51 Customs Duty Calculation

All countries that are members of the World Trade Organization (WTO) abide by customs value calculation rules adopted by WTO. These rules are enumerated in article VII of the GATT (General agreement on Tariffs and Trade). Uniform and transparent customs-value calculation rules prevent arbitrariness in determining customs duties to be paid to the authorities and prevent duty evasion by importers. Transaction values form the basis for customs value calculation under the GATT rules. Transaction value is essentially the gross invoice price less discounts. These rules also specify what kind of costs can be added to and subtracted from transaction values in order to arrive at customs value.

Customs duties are paid by importers on goods imported into a country. For the most part, duties are ad valorem duties; i.e., they are assessed as a certain percent, called the duty rate, of the customs value. Less frequently used are specific duties that are assessed based on quantity of imports or number of line items, without respect to the value of the goods.

In GTS, customs duties are calculated in the customs-shipment document based on the configuration rules for customs-value calculation and customs-duty rates set up in the system.

▶ **Configuring Customs Duty Calculation**
Customs duty calculation is configured in the implementation guide (Transaction SPRO) under Customs Management (see Figure 5.52).

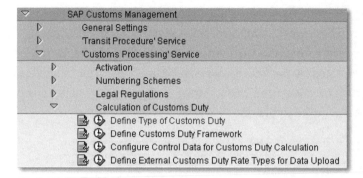

Figure 5.52 Configuring Customs Duty Calculation in Implementation Guide

▶ **Define Type of Customs Duty**

Customs duty types are used to configure all categories of line items that go into a custom duty calculation, including customs values, total, subtotals, and various types of duties. Settings in the customs duty, such as duty type, control its behavior in the overall calculation. Transportation costs shown in Figure 5.53 have a duty category of A0 Transaction amount; this is an item that is added to or subtracted from transaction amount to come up with customs value. Maintenance level of Duty Type determines if it is maintained at header or item. If it is maintained at header level, Distribution Type determines whether it is distributed to items by weight or value.

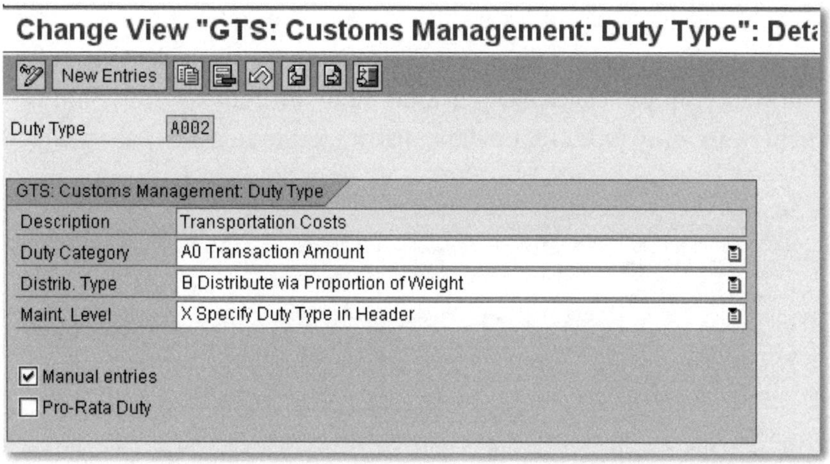

Figure 5.53 Duty Type Definition

Custom Duty Framework

Customs Duty Framework combines, for a given legal regulation, all customs duty types in a numbered sequence based on the rules of the duty calculation enumerated by the authorities (see Figure 5.54). The framework is a representation of calculation rules shown in Figure 5.51, using customs duty types as the building blocks.

L.Reg.	SeqNo	Duty		Value Type
ACE	10	A001 Value of Goods		001 Net Price/Invoice Value
ACE	20	A002 Transportation Costs		Value not Shown Separately
ACE	30	A003 Insurance Costs		Value not Shown Separately
ACE	40	C100 Customs Value		002 Customs Value
ACE	70	B200 Preferential Customs Duty		Value not Shown Separately
ACE	80	B100 Third-Country Duty		Value not Shown Separately
ACE	100	C001 Total of Customs Value + Duties		Value not Shown Separately
ACE	110	D001 Total Duties		Value not Shown Separately
ACE	140	W001 Value for Foreign Trade Statist…		003 Statistical Value

Figure 5.54 Customs Duty Framework

► **Calculation Profile**

Calculation profiles are assigned to combinations of customs document type and legal regulation to influence the calculation of customs duties. Calculation profile is assigned exclusion requirements that control whether certain duty types are not considered in duty calculation under certain conditions, for example in case of customer returns (see Figure 5.55). Calculation profiles are also assigned "completeness rules" to make sure all the elements required for calculating are available. Such rules, for instance, might check that customs value or item weight is not zero if there are duty types that will be distributed to items based on weight.

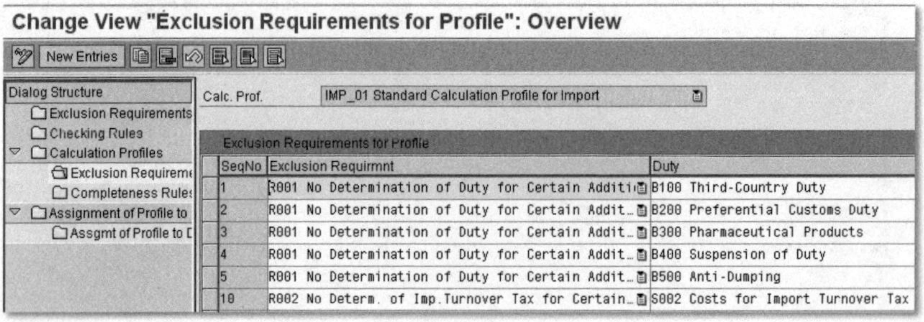

Change View "Exclusion Requirements for Profile": Overview

New Entries

Dialog Structure	Calc. Prof.	IMP_01 Standard Calculation Profile for Import	
☐ Exclusion Requirements			
☐ Checking Rules			
▽ ☐ Calculation Profiles		Exclusion Requirements for Profile	
☐ Exclusion Requireme	SeqNo	Exclusion Requirmnt	Duty
☐ Completeness Rule	1	R001 No Determination of Duty for Certain Additi…	B100 Third-Country Duty
▽ ☐ Assignment of Profile to	2	R001 No Determination of Duty for Certain Addit…	B200 Preferential Customs Duty
☐ Assgmt of Profile to C	3	R001 No Determination of Duty for Certain Addit…	B300 Pharmaceutical Products
	4	R001 No Determination of Duty for Certain Addit…	B400 Suspension of Duty
	5	R001 No Determination of Duty for Certain Addit…	B500 Anti-Dumping
	10	R002 No Determ. of Imp.Turnover Tax for Certain…	S002 Costs for Import Turnover Tax

Figure 5.55 Calculation Profile Exclusion Requirements

▶ **Customs Duty Calculation in Shipment Document**

Customs duties are calculated in the shipment document based on the configuration of the Customs Duty Framework and the duty rates maintained in the system. Duty rates can be uploaded using data files from data providers, or you can maintain duty rates manually using transaction /SAPSLL/TLC_CUSB (see Figure 5.56).

| List | Edit | Goto | Environment | System | Help |

Display: Duty Rates for Period -

Legal Regulation: TIACE US Automated Customs Environment (ACE)

Cust.Tariff No.	Duty	CountOrgGr	De...	Valid from	Valid to	...	Amount	Curr...	/	UoM	Percentage
8501104040	B200	NAFTA	US	06/26/2006	01/01/2010	3			0		0.000
8501104040	B200	USMFN	US	01/01/2006	01/01/4000	3			0		2.900
8501104060	B200	NAFTA	US	01/01/2006	01/01/4000	3			0		0.000
8501104060	B200	USMFN	US	06/26/2006	01/01/2010	3			0		2.900

Figure 5.56 Customs Duty Rates

Customs tariff numbers are the basis for duty maintenance. Customs authorities publish duty rates applicable for tariff code (HTS code in the U.S.). The HTS code assigned to a product under a customs legal regulation, along with the product country of origin on the shipment document, is used by the system to determine the applicable duty rate.

Customs shipment document triggered by the R/3 billing document or R/3 goods receipt gets the invoice value or the value of goods from the backend system. Duty rates and calculation rules maintained in GTS are applied to the value received from R/3 (see Figure 5.57). Customs values calculated in the shipment document are used in electronic declarations made to customs agencies.

This concludes the discussion of the customs-duty calculation functionality in GTS. We looked at the basic principle behind customs duty calculation as mandated by WTO rules and the configuration options available to implement those rules in GTS. In Section 5.3, we will discuss the Transit Procedure Service.

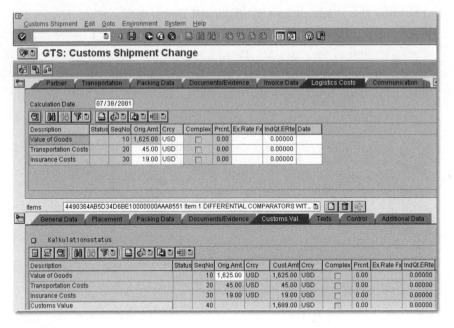

Figure 5.57 Customs Duty Calculation on a Customs Shipment Document

5.3 Transit Procedure Service

Goods movement within the EU and the European Free Trade Association (EFTA) as well as exports to and from EU countries are facilitated by the New Computerized Transit System (NCTS). NCTS enables electronic declarations processing, eliminating the need for slow and inefficient paper-based procedures. Streamlined electronic procedures involve electronic presentment of transit information to customs offices of departure and destination.

In some cases, this eliminates the need for physical presentation of goods, allowing direct movement from origin to destination. NCTS was developed by the European Union with a central server in Brussels and access for traders from any Web-connected PC. However, for companies with heavy volume, the Web option is impractical because of dual entry of data in internal systems and then into NCTS. The GTS Customs module provides certified software for connecting to NCTS using EDI translator software from Seeburger Inc.

5.3.1 Transit Procedure Business Process

Exports and imports in the EU and transit within EU can be electronically declared using the NCTS. This is accomplished by sending and receiving pre defined electronic messages in EDIFACT format with relevant customs offices.

Export of goods from the EU involves sending an electronic export declaration to the customs office of export, which may be an in-country office. These goods are again presented to the office of exit at the border. Transit of goods to EU or EFTA countries on the other hand, is simplified by not requiring goods to be presented to the office of exit. Furthermore, there are two possible transit-procedure business flows, which we will discuss next.

Normal Procedure

Normal procedure involves declaring a transit procedure to the customs office of departure and receiving clearance from that office. Goods are then transported directly to the office of destination under bond, without presentation at an office of exit. NCTS enables the normal procedure with electronic exchange of messages between the trader and the office of departure, as shown in Figure 5.58

Simplified Procedure

For authorized consignors and authorized consignees, the transit procedure is further simplified by eliminating the need to present goods at either the office of departure or of destination. All formalities are completed via electronic messages;goods presentation happens at the trader location, not at the customs office. See Figure 5.59 for an illustration of the exchange of electronic messages between the parties involved in a simplified procedure.

Now that we have looked at the business process for transit procedures, let's look at the configuration required in GTS for enabling this process.

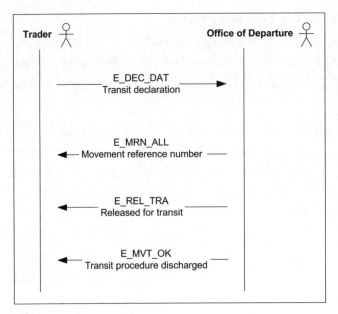

Figure 5.58 NCTS Normal Transit Procedure EDIFACT Messages

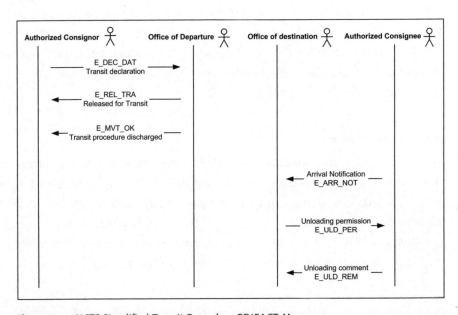

Figure 5.59 NCTS Simplified Transit Procedure EDIFACT Messages

5.3.2 Configuring Transit Procedure Service

Transit Procedure Service generates messages for communicating with NCTS from a customs shipment document. Customs shipment documents can be either manually created in GTS or triggered for creation from a back-end R/3 document. For outbound goods movement, a customs shipment document can be triggered by R/3 billing document. For an inbound goods movement, it can be triggered by an R/3 inbound delivery document.

Transit Procedure Service shares most of the configuration steps that have been enumerated for the customs processing service earlier. These can be seen in the subsequent sub-sections.

Legal Regulation

Legal regulation forms the basis of activating any services, and in GTS this includes the transit procedure service. Legal regulations for transit procedure are created with a law code of **07**.

Post Processing Framework

PPF provides the basis for the messages that are sent to and received from customs offices. GTS delivered configuration provides process templates for EU country specific NCTS messages (see Figure 5.60)

Process Templ.	TRSNL	Transit - Netherlands (NCTS)
Process	TRS0	Open Transit Procedure
Process Activit	NLNVA	Normal Procedure

| Messages | |
Message	Description
NL215	NL: Transit Declaration
NLI09	NL: Cancellation Decision
NLI16	NL: Transit Declaration Rejection
NLI28	NL: Formal Acceptance
NLI29	NL: Release for Transit
NLI51	NL: No Release for Transit
NLI60	NL: Inspection Required
TRNSY	NL: CONTRL Message - EDI Syntax Error

Figure 5.60 Process Template for Netherlands NCTS Messages

Document Structure

Setting up a document structure for Transit Procedure Service involves customs document type and customs item category definition. These are followed by assignment of back-end R/3 document types to the customs document type and item category that will trigger the creation of transit documents in GTS. Assignment of an action profile to the customs document type and legal regulation combination is the link between the PPF and messages for transit procedure service (see Figure 5.61).

| Customs Doc.Typ | TRLOEX | Customs Shipment (Transit): Export | |
| Legal Reg. | TRSNL | (NCTS) Transit Procedure The Netherlands | |

Control Settings for Document Type / Legal Regulation		
Action Profile	LLS_NL_TR_EX	GTS: Dutch Profile for Transit (Export)
Partner Group	P6CTRO	Partner Group for 'Transit' Service - Export
TextDetermProc.	SLL_CD_GEN	Customs Document - General
Calc. Prof.	EXP_01	Standard Calculation Profile for Export

Figure 5.61 Action Profile Assignment to Transit Procedure Legal Regulation

Custom Code Lists

Custom code lists are the list of acceptable values on the EDI messages that are sent to NCTS. National customs authorities publish acceptable values for the following:

▸ Means of transport
▸ Declaration types
▸ Package types
▸ Seal types

You can maintain these values in custom code lists. When customs shipment documents are created, only the acceptable values maintained in these custom code lists are available for entry and ultimately for sending on the EDI message to NCTS.

Numbering Scheme

The customs product master has to be classified with an EU eight-digit combined nomenclature (CN) code that is based on the HS. For this purpose, you need to maintain a numbering scheme for the combined nomenclature that can be assigned to transit procedure legal regulations. The CN code assigned to the product master then is defaulted into the customs shipment document and sent on the EDI message to NCTS.

Control Settings for Transit procedure Service

In this configuration step, you assign a process template to transit procedure legal regulation. This is the link between the legal regulation and the different messages that can be sent to and received from NCTS for customs-shipment documents processed under that legal regulation.

To enable simplified procedures, you need to maintain authorization types for the role your company will be playing: authorized consignor or authorized consignee. In using the Transit Procedure Service, you then need to maintain the actual authorizations you have received from the customs authorities as licenses in GTS. Customs-shipment documents check these authorizations to make sure they are current. Similarly, you need to configure guarantees so you can maintain securities in the system. These securities are used as a bond given to the customs office for allowing the goods movement.

5.3.3 Transit Declarations

Transit declarations are made on the basis of a customs shipment document that can be either manually created or triggered from a back-end R/3 document. After the creation of the customs shipment, the document goes through consistency checks to make sure all the elements required for an EDI message to NCTS are present. Checks include presence of valid office of departure and office of transit, guarantee validity, etc. After passing these checks, transit declaration message is generated and transmitted to NCTS (see Figure 5.62).

You need to create customs office of departure and transit ahead of time as business partners and maintain their external office numbers. You also need to maintain the EDI partner profile for the customs office using message type /SAPSLL/TRS_DEC for outbound transit messages and /SAPSLL/TRS_INBOUND for inbound transit messages. You need to maintain securities to be used by customs authorities as guarantees in GTS.

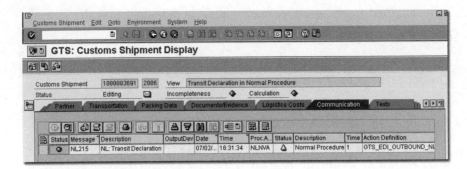

Figure 5.62 Transit Declaration Message

5.4 Conclusion

In this chapter we discussed the functionality within the Customs Management module in GTS. We discussed the configuration of the Customs Processing Service and the Transit Procedure Service, printing of standard customs forms, and calculation of customs duties.

The comprehensive nature of customs functionality available in GTS can enable automation and improve the speed at which your company clears shipments through customs, which can be leveraged by your company as a competitive advantage in the marketplace. In Chapter 6, we will delve into the GTS Risk Management module.

In this chapter, we will focus on the Risk Management module in GTS. We will cover the building blocks of preference processing with respect to NAFTA and the EU, including building preference-determination rule sets and processing vendor declarations. This chapter also addresses restitution management with respect to the EU Common Agricultural Policy.

6 Risk Management

The Risk Management module of GTS comprises of two main services, both dedicated to the management of a specific trade process. These two services are Preference Processing and Restitution Processing. The Risk Management module helps manage trade processes that pose a financial risk to your company. Trade preference processing in preference zones like the North American Free Trade Agreement (NAFTA) or the European Union (EU) has a direct impact on the bottom line of your company. For example, manufacturing or sourcing products from within the preference zones can make your company more competitive as a supplier. Restitution Management can help EU companies that provide agricultural or processed-food products claim direct restitution payments, which in turn can make their products competitive outside of the EU. Let's look at these two in more detail now.

6.1 Preference Processing

Preference processing is the process of claiming preferred import duty rates for your company's products, certifying eligibility under the rules of origin specified by the trade agreement between participating countries.

The GTS Preference Processing service deals with customs tariff preferences available under major trade agreements. Most major multilateral trade alliances like NAFTA or the EU have customs tariff preferences available for products originating in the countries that are part of the trade agreement. Preferential duties for originating products can be as low as 0%, thus constituting a major competitive advantage for exporters trying to sell to companies in the preference zone countries. This is because customers buying products that are eligible for preferential duty rates can significantly reduce their costs, especially in industries such as retail where customs import duties make up a major part of overall product costs.

There are complex rules of eligibility for claiming preferential duty rates, and these are designed to stimulate economic activity in the countries that are part of the trade agreement. In general, to claim originating goods status within a preference zone, the goods have to be either fully produced within the participating countries—including raw materials and parts—or have more than the threshold regional value specified in the rules

In the context of NAFTA, if an exporter is producing goods that are made of raw materials, components, ingredients that originate fully in NAFTA, the exporter can claim NAFTA origin for its goods and be eligible for preferential duty rates going into U.S., Canada, or Mexico. In this case, the exporter can use the NAFTA certificate of origin as the document for claiming preference.

In case the goods are made of materials or parts that are non-NAFTA, there are rules specified in the Annex 401 of the NAFTA agreement for determining eligibility to claim preference. Typically, this involves an analysis of the composition of the product based on product specific rules of origin.

6.1.1   Rules of Origin

Rules of origin are written into trade-preference agreements to give a recipe to the exporters to determine whether their goods can claim preference. In the case of NAFTA and other agreements, these rules are based on the Harmonized Tariff System (HTS), which is also the basis for levying customs duties. Trade preference rules take the following forms:

Tariff Shift

This means that after obtaining the HTS classification for the final product the exporter needs to analyze the non-originating components' or materials' HTS classifications. In the process to produce the final product in the region, there has to be a tariff shift; i.e.,the HTS classification of the final product has to be different from those of its non-originating components.

Regional Value Content

This is another method used in determining preference status. Simply stated, this means that the process to produce the goods in the preference zone countries should add value to the end product in excess of the value of the non-originating value.

Specific Production Process

In some cases the preference rules may specify a specific procedure (e.g., sanding, refinement, etc.) to have been performed in the region for a product to be eligible to claim preferential status.

The rules of origin are usually written as a combination of the above three types of requirements. Figure 6.1 shows rules of origin from NAFTA Annex 401, for a product that can be classified under the HTS headings of 8407 through 8408.

84.07– 84.08[16]	A change to heading 84.07 through 84.08 from any other heading, including another heading within that group, provided there is a regional value content of not less than: (a) 60 percent where the transaction value method is used, or (b) 50 percent where the net cost method is used.

Figure 6.1 NAFTA Rules of Origin for HTS Heading 8407 Through 8408

The HTS number is used to identify a product to the customs authorities. It is a 10-digit hierarchical number with each digit having some significance, as explained below. The 10 digits of HTS number break down as follows:

▶ Chapter: two digits
▶ Heading: four digits

- ▸ Subheading: six digits;
- ▸ Tariff item: eight digits
- ▸ Statistical break: ten digits

The rule, as seen in Figure 6.1, can be used by an exporter that is analyzing preference eligibility for a product that is classified with a complete 10-digit HTS number whose first four digits are 8407 through 8408. The rule can be interpreted to mean that the non-originating materials that constitute the final product must be classified with an HTS number whose first four digits are not 8407 through 8408. The value of the regional materials or processes must be greater than 60 % of transaction value or more than 50 % of invoice value less transport, packaging, insurance, and other costs.

Naturally, if the materials are wholly produced within NAFTA using NAFTA originating materials, the exporter can directly issue a NAFTA certificate of origin under NAFTA Criterion C.

6.1.2 Preference Processing in GTS

Preference processing in GTS involves the following:

- ▸ Configuring the rules for preference determination
- ▸ Transferring the bill of material (BOM) for the product for which you want to determine preferential status
- ▸ Classifying materials with an HTS number
- ▸ Maintaining vendor declarations for externally procured components of a BOM
- ▸ Transfer of billing or order documents from back-end R/3 system to establish regional value content
- ▸ Transfer of purchasing documents and goods receipts to generate vendor declaration requests for your vendors
- ▸ Configuring preference-determination rules

Rules for preference determination can be configured manually in the implementation guide (Transaction SPRO) or they can be loaded via XML files from data providers.

To build preference rules manually in the system, GTS provides constructs such as procedures, procedure groups, and rule groups to link conditions. In order to configure the NAFTA preference rule shown in Figure 6.1, you would have to create the following:

▶ A preference procedure called **Tariff shift** numbered 00001 in this example, as seen in Figure 6.2.

▶ A preference procedure called **Regional Value content** numbered 00002 in this example, also shown in Figure 6.2.

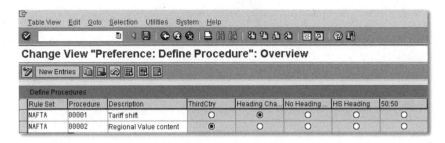

Figure 6.2 Procedure for Preference Rules

▶ Group the two procedures together with an **AND** (since both conditions have to be satisfied) in a Procedure Group (see Figure 6.3).

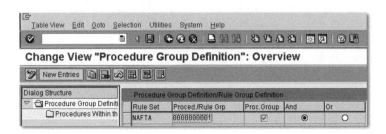

Figure 6.3 Procedure Group

▶ The procedures in the group need to have further detail added. For procedure 00001, 100 % tariff shift should occur in the final product; therefore you specify the operand **EQ** and percentage **100** (see Figure 6.4). For procedure 00002, regional value content must be at least 60 %, or stated negatively, non-regional content must be less than or equal to 40 %. Therefore, you specify the operand **LE** and percentage **40** (see Figure 6.5) in the procedure group.

Rule Set	NAFTA	NAFTA preference processing	
Rule Group	0000000001	"And" Operation	
Seq.No. Proced.	1		
Pref. Procedure	00001 7	Tariff shift	
Seq.No.TariffNo	0		

Procedures Within the Group

Cust.Tariff No.	
Incl./Excl.	
Operation Code	EQ Equal to
Perc.Share	100.00

Figure 6.4 Procedure Group for Tariff Shift

Rule Set	NAFTA	NAFTA preference processing	
Rule Group	0000000001	"And" Operation	
Seq.No. Proced.	2		
Pref. Procedure	00002...	Regional Value content	
Seq.No.TariffNo	0		

Procedures Within the Group

Cust.Tariff No.	
Incl./Excl.	
Operation Code	LE Smaller than or equal to
Perc.Share	40.00

Figure 6.5 Procedure Group for Regional Value Content

▶ Assign the rule group to the NAFTA preference agreement.

▶ Assign the rule group to the tariff heading. In this example, this would be 8407 and 8408 HTS headings (see Figure 6.6).

After configuring preference-determination rules, you can run preference determination on your products, which can mark them as being eligible for lowered duties. Let's look at these in more detail.

Vendor Declarations

You need to maintain vendor declarations for the components that go into your final product. These declarations are furnished by your vendors certifying either preferential status or a negative preferential status with a certain percentage of local content that can be used in your own preference determination.

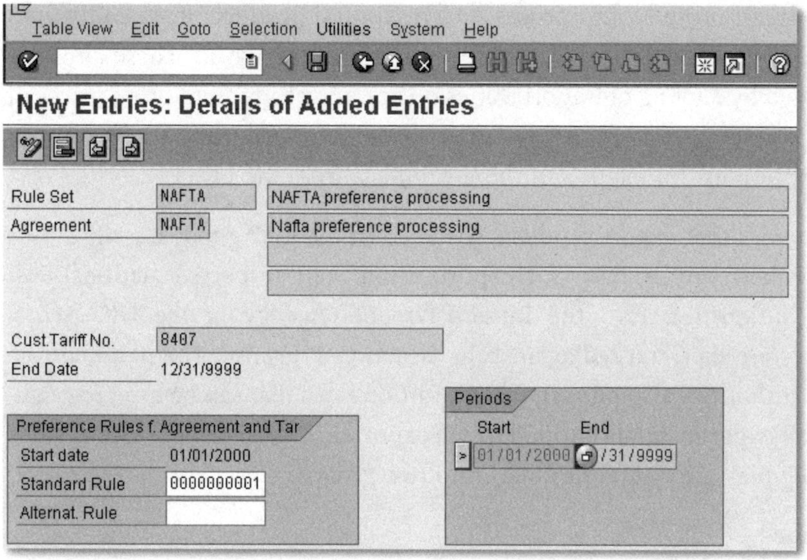

Figure 6.6 Assignment of Rule Group to Tariff Heading

GTS enables the process of requesting and maintaining vendor declarations, including generating request letters to your vendors, keeping track of expiry of declarations, and sending reminders to your vendors.

Preference Determination

Preference determination can be run in GTS using the rules uploaded or configured manually into the system. A preference-determination run can determine if your product is eligible for preferential treatment under the rules and sets a preference indicator in the customs product master. If there are regional value content requirements in the rules, preference determination also establishes a minimum price at which the product can be sold without compromising its eligibility.

Billing documents transferred from the back-end R/3 system are checked to see if the price is more than the minimum price in the customs product master. If it is, GTS sets a preference indicator in the R/3 document.

6.2 ˙ Restitution Processing

Restitution processing in GTS enables the management of the EU's Common Agricultural Policy (CAP) restitution process. CAP is designed to keep agricultural produce and processed agricultural products from companies in the EU competitive with those in the rest of the world. These aims are achieved by levying of import duties on specific products to bring prices of these products up to EU levels and by providing restitution in the form of export refunds for exports of these products from the EU.

Companies that export products specified in the CAP goods classifications can request CAP licenses for exports from their respective national customs authorities; e.g., the Rural Payments Agency in the UK. Actual exports are then tracked against the issued CAP license. The national customs authorities also publish the restitution rates that can be used to calculate the export refunds entitled to the exporter of these goods. CAP divides the eligible agricultural products into two groups:

▶ **Annex 1**
These goods consist of agricultural produce; e.g., apples, pears, etc.

▶ **Non-Annex 1**
These goods are processed agricultural products such as sugar, milk, eggs, confectionary, etc.

Products that are eligible for CAP restitution are identified by their CAP classification numbers. The CAP classification number borrows its first eight digits from the Combined Nomenclature of the EU, which in turn borrows its first six digits from the Harmonized System (HS). The CAP number comprises the eight digits of the combined nomenclature, plus four digits.

6.2.1 ˙ Restitution Processing in GTS

To enable restitution processing in GTS, all relevant customs product masters need to be assigned the 12-digit CAP list number. You need to maintain the CAP licenses approved for your company in GTS with the CAP list numbers and the quantity approved for receiving export refunds. When a billing document is created in the R/3 back-end system for CAP-eligible product, it is transferred to GTS as a customs document that looks for and deducts the quantity from the CAP license.

You need to store the export refund rates for the combination of CAP list number and the destination country that are published by the national customs authorities. These rates can be used to calculate the refunds that are due to your company.

In general, the Restitution Processing service in GTS works on the same principle as the export compliance. The concept of determination strategy and licenses are carried over into this part of GTS.

6.2.2 Configuring Restitution Processing

All settings in this section need to be made in the implementation guide (Transaction SPRO), **Global Trade Services · Risk Management · Restitution Service · Legal regulation for restitution processing**.

You need to configure a legal regulation for restitution processing using the law code of "08" for CAP law, as seen in Figure 6.7.

Legal Regulation	EUCAP
Legal Regulation	
Description	EU Common Agricultural policy
Type of law code	08 Restitution
Import/Export	2 Export/Dispatch
Origin ctry-Leg.reg.	

Figure 6.7 Legal Regulation for Restitution Processing

Activate the legal regulation for all departure countries in the EU where your company has a Legal Unit. In other words, if you have a plant in Britain and Germany that ships CAP-eligible products, you need to activate the legal regulation for both country codes GB and DE.

Activate Restitution Service

You need to activate the customs document types and item categories that are relevant for restitution processing. Back-end R/3 sales orders and billing documents that map to customs documents in GTS would need to be activated for restitution service. You also need to activate the legal regulation for the departure countries in EU.

Numbering Scheme for CAP

Key to the functioning of the CAP restitution process is that all relevant products need to be classified with a CAP goods-list number. For this purpose, you need to configure a CAP numbering scheme (see Figure 6.8) that can be populated with both Annex I and Non-Annex I numbers and then be used to classify a customs product master restitution view.

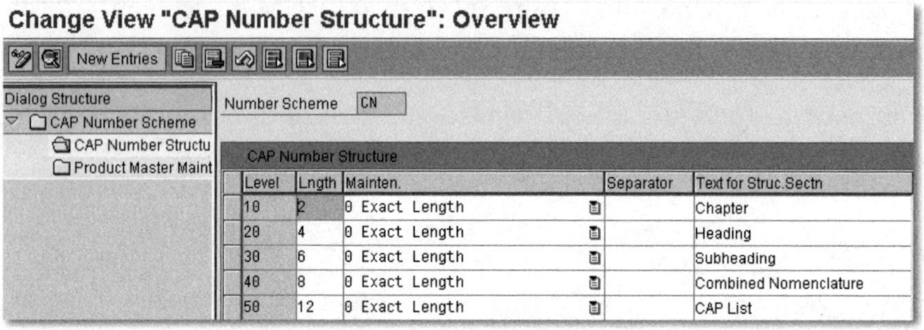

Figure 6.8 CAP List Numbering Scheme

Control Settings for Restitution Processing Service

Control settings for the Restitution Processing service control the behavior of the service with respect to the level at which the determination strategy is maintained. Figure 6.9 shows the license strategy to be maintained at country group and control class, which in this case means CAP goods-list number. Next, you need to assign the determination procedure to the restitution legal regulation (see Figure 6.10).

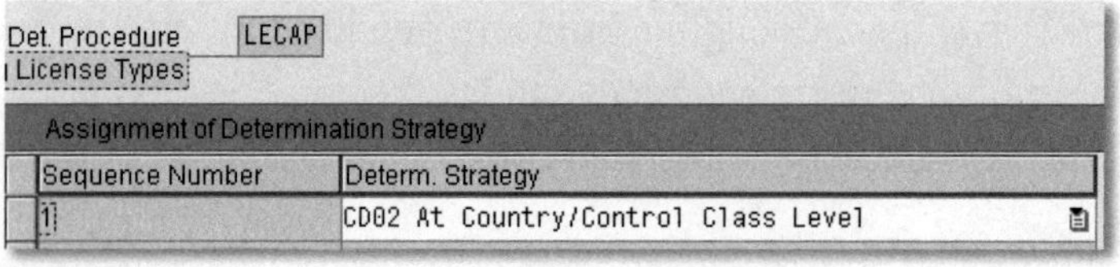

Figure 6.9 Determination Procedure for CAP License

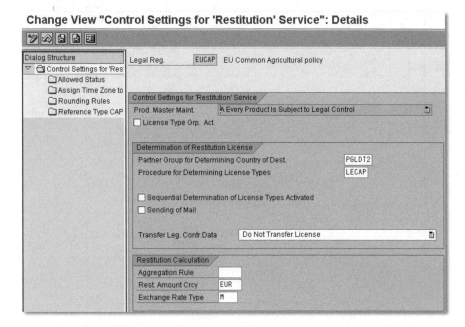

Figure 6.10 Assign Determination Procedure to Restitution Legal Regulation

Define Restitution License Types

Restitution licenses need to be maintained in GTS to make sure sales orders and billing documents contain consuming quantities approved by the customs authorities. Licenses are applied for fixed quantities of products identified by their Combined Nomenclature number, as shown in Figure 6.11.

You need to create the license structure from Figure 6.11 in GTS as a restitution license type (see Figure 6.12) with attributes **CAP Number**, **Dep/Dest Cty** (departure or destination country), and **Quantity Update**.

Define Recipe Type

For Non-Annex I CAP goods—i.e., processed agricultural products—you need to create a recipe, which means that a recipe type has to be defined. Non-Annex I goods are processed agricultural products that are made from agricultural products that are eligible for restitution. An example is confectionary products like cakes that have sugar, milk, and eggs as ingredients. The recipe for the processed agricultural product simply identifies the ingredients, thus helping calculate restitution for the end product.

EUROPEAN COMMUNITY — EXPORT LICENCE OR ADVANCE FIXING CERTIFICATE A G R E X

2

ISSUING AGENCY'S COPY

1 Agency issuing the licence or certificate (name and address)

2 Issuing agency's emboss-ment and perforation (¹)

No /

3

4 Issued (name, full address and Member State)

5 Agency issuing the extract (name and address)

6 Rights transferred to

with effect from

Stamp of the competent agency:

7 Receiving country

Compulsory YES NO

8 Advance fixing requested YES NO

9 Tendering requested YES NO

10 Date of lodging original licence/ certificate application

11 Total amount of security

12 LAST DAY OF VALIDITY

2

13 PRODUCT TO BE EXPORTED

14 Trade in figures

15 Description in accordance with the Combined Nomenclature (CN)

16 CN code(s)

17 Quantity (¹) in figures

18 Quantity (¹) in words

19 Tolerance % more

20 Special particulars

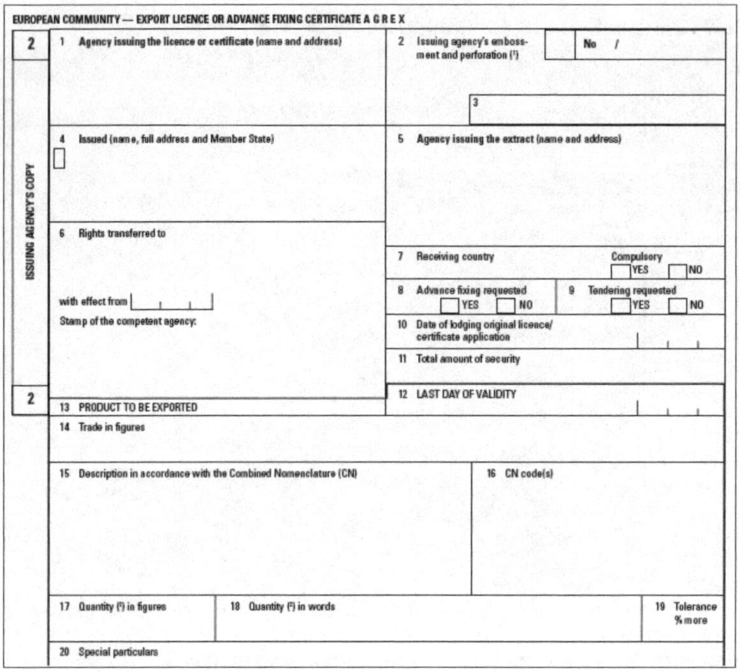

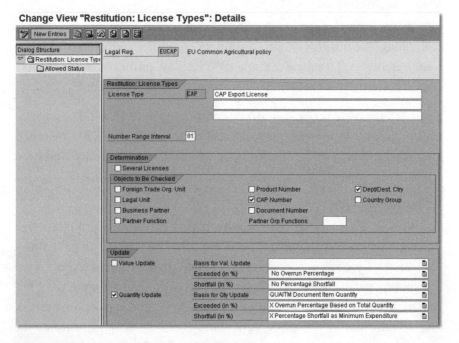

Figure 6.11 CAP License Application

Figure 6.12 Restitution License Type Definition

6.2.3 Business Process of Restitution Processing

In order to use the restitution service with the back-end R/3 documents, you must put in place the master data that it needs to work with.

Maintain CAP Goods List Numbers

You can either manually maintain CAP list numbers that will be used to classify the CAP eligible products or load XML files with this data from data providers. Transaction /SAPSLL/LLNS_802 is used for maintaining CAP numbers, as can be seen in Figure 6.13.

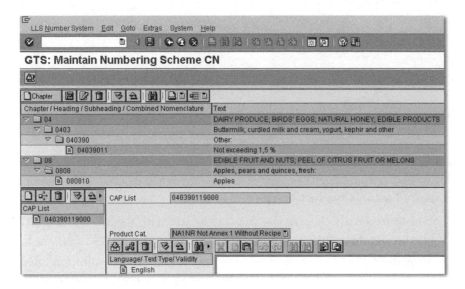

Figure 6.13 Maintain CAP List Numbers

Create Recipes for Non-Annex I Products

Create recipes for Non-Annex I products indicating the agricultural ingredients that are eligible for restitution under CAP and their proportion in the end product (See Figure 6.14). Use transaction /SAPSLL/BOP02.

These recipes can be registered with the relevant national customs authorities (e.g., the Rural Payments Agency in the UK) to expedite the process of getting refunds for exports of these products.

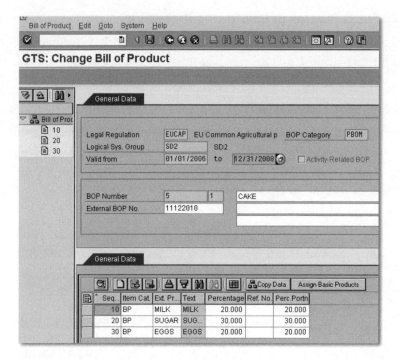

Figure 6.14 Recipe for Non-Annex I Products

Classify Customs Product Master

You need to classify the customs product master with the appropriate CAP goods-list number. This classification will be the basis for GTS to assign the appropriate CAP license and to calculate refunds based on restitution rates. In case of non-Annex I products, you also need to assign the recipe to the end product (see Figure 6.15).

Create CAP Licenses

Create approved CAP licenses in the restitution master data, using transaction /SAPSLL/LCLICR02. Add the CAP number, destination country, and the quantity for which the license was approved as shown in Figure 6.16.

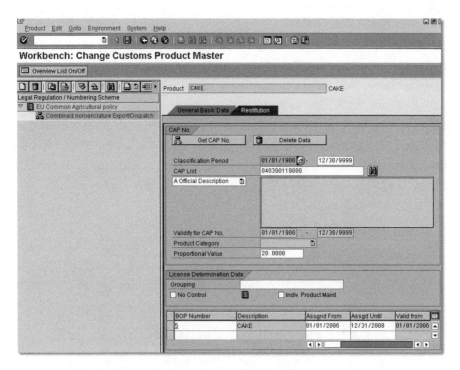

Figure 6.15 Classify Customs Product Master with CAP Goods List Number

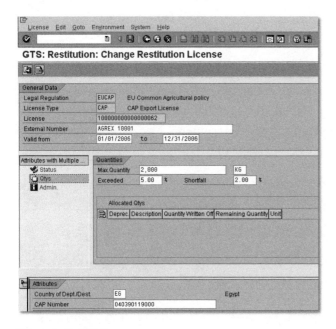

Figure 6.16 CAP License

Maintain Restitution Rates

Restitution rates allow you to calculate export refunds due to your company. These rates are published by national customs authorities and can be maintained in the system if you want to calculate refunds. The maintenance of the restitution rates is of importance to the refund-calculation functionality in GTS. When billing documents are transferred from the back-end R/3 system for CAP-eligible shipments, GTS can use these rates to calculate restitution that can be claimed for each shipment, as shown in Figure 6.17.

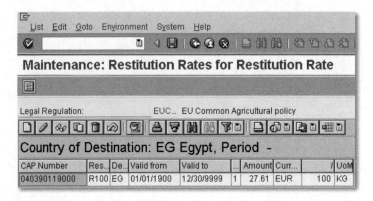

Figure 6.17 Restitution Refund Rates

Monitor Restitution Documents

Customs document types that are activated for restitution are assigned CAP licenses in a way very similar to the assignment of export licenses in the Compliance module. Monitoring of documents blocked for restitution is done using transaction /SAPSLL/RES_BLCD, as seen in Figure 6.18.

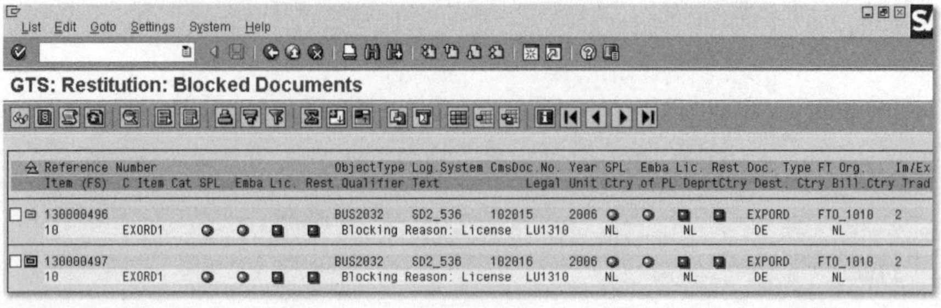

Figure 6.18 Restitution Blocked Documents

6.3   Conclusion

In this chapter we talked about the Risk Management module in GTS. We discussed the business process for preference processing under agreements like NAFTA and functionality available in GTS to enable some of those processes. We stressed that preference determination in GTS is a key to making your products competitive under NAFTA or EU by leveraging origin rules and lowered import duties on eligible products.

We also covered vendor declarations that your company can make to your customers, which in turn can be used by them to claim those lowered import duties from customs. To round out the vendor-declaration process, GTS functionality can also enable you as a customer to keep track of declarations from your own vendors.

In addition, we discussed the restitution process under the Common Agricultural Policy of the European Union and its implementation in the Restitution Processing service in GTS. We discussed the role of GTS in the entire end- to-end business process related to restitution: from maintaining recipes for non-Annex I products, to maintenance of restitution rates, to calculation and tracking of export refunds due to your company.

This chapter concludes the discussion of all the major modules and their services in GTS. In Chapter 7, we will cover important, miscellaneous topics, such as connecting and using SPL service with non-R/3 back-end systems, archiving, and the differences between GTS 3.0 and GTS 7.0.

In this final chapter, we will focus on a variety of topics that involve the use of GTS services such as SPL screening for non R/3 systems, archiving of documents, and the differences between GTS 3.0 and 7.0

7   Miscellaneous Issues

Thus far, we have looked at all the major modules in GTS, the functionality offered, the business context for implementing that functionality, and also the implementation steps. After you have implemented GTS, you will want to leverage your investment in the product and get the most out of it.

This chapter introduces you to some of the ways you can get the most out of your GTS implementation. For instance, after you have integrated GTS SPL screening service with the R/3 back end, you may have other applications with customer, vendor, employee, or contacts information that need SPL screening to comply with export laws. This chapter shows you how to expose SPL screening to non R/3 systems.

After your GTS implementation has been live for some time, archiving of data in GTS is critical to ensure proper functioning of the system. This chapter introduces you to the standard archiving objects available in GTS.

In this chapter, I also write about the changes needed in R/3 to interrupt the sales order or the purchase order to delivery process of your supply chain if GTS blocks a document because of compliance problems.

We also will explain the differences between the functionality possible with GTS 7.0 and which is available in GTS 3.0.

7.1   SPL Screening for Non-SAP Systems

Sanctioned Party List (SPL) screening is required by U.S. export administration regulations to prevent dealings with entities on the denied-party lists put out by various government agencies. GTS SPL functionality is designed to work with non-R/3 back-end systems. A number of major corporations choose a heterogeneous application environment that includes best-of breed solutions from different vendors. Besides legacy applications that have information needing SPL screening. GTS is designed to be a central engine for providing SPL screening services to non R/3 applications that may exist in a corporation's enterprise applications environment.

Government regulations govern the screening of different types of parties involved in doing business with your company, including customers, vendors, employees, and parties involved in financial transactions. GTS can provide SPL screening services to screen these entities from both R/3 and non R/3 systems. We have already covered SPL screening for R/3 systems in Chapter 3; here we will examine SPL screening for non-R/3 legacy system. Considerations that go into using GTS SPL screening with a non R/3 system are discussed now.

7.1.1   SPL Screening Function Module

GTS provides a function module specifically written for use with non R/3 systems. Function module /SAPSLL/SPL_SCENARIO_S3_RFC is a Remote Function Call (RFC)-enabled function module that accepts any element of the name and address of an entity and screens it using the rules configured in GTS to return matches to sanctioned parties found in the SPL master data.

7.1.2   Method of Accessing GTS

GTS SPL screening functionality can be exposed to a non-R/3 system in a variety of ways. Depending on the capabilities of the interfacing system, you can choose from among the menu of methods available. One such method is exposing the SPL screening function module as a Web service.

7.1.3   SPL Screening Web Service

A Web service is a software application that is accessed via standard XML messages over a network. Web service use has two sides: a Web service, (also called the Web-service provider),and a Web-service client that consumes the service. Web service use is governed by a set of standards that all providers and consumers adhere to. SAP Web Application Server 6.40 onwards provides a standard way of converting any RFC-enabled function module as a Web service.

For non-R/3 systems that comprehend Web services and are capable of acting as a Web service client have the option of exposing the SPL screening function module as a Web service. To create a Web service for the SPL screening function module, perform the following steps:

1. Create a Web service for SPL function module /SAPSLL/SPL_SCENARIO_ S3_RFC using the Web-service creation wizard, transaction WS_WZD_ START, as shown in Figure 7.1.

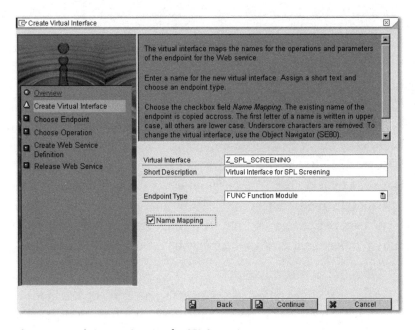

Figure 7.1 Web Service Creation for SPL Screening

2. Test the SPL Web service from the Web-service home page generated by the wizard, as seen in Figure 7.2 on the next page.

3. Publish the Web Service Definition Language (WSDL) for the SPL-screening Web service.

4. Consume the SPL Web service from non R/3 applications using the generated WSDL.

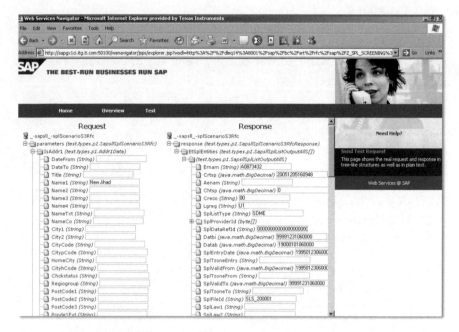

Figure 7.2 SPL Screening Web Service Test

7.1.4 Dedicated Application Server for Non-R/3 Applications

In a heterogeneous application environment, where SAP R/3 coexists with other legacy applications that require SPL screening services from GTS, you may need to dedicate GTS application servers to each application. Having separate GTS application servers ensures that mission-critical business processes that require robust SPL screening are not impacted by the demands of other applications, which may be the case with shared application servers.

Using separate GTS application servers entails repetition of SPL index creation and load jobs on each application server. In other words, SPL data files need to be loaded to all application server separately, followed by the index creation on each server. In a multiple-application server scenario, the SPL- screening Web service can be deployed on the application server meant for the legacy application without impacting R/3 performance.

For example, in your GTS implementation you can have application server APP01 dedicated to R/3, while application server APP02 is dedicated to SPL-screening services for non-R/3 systems.

7.2   R/3 Copy Control Changes for Compliance Management

The Compliance Management module in GTS blocks documents that fail compliance checks activated for back-end R/3 documents. Changes to R/3 copy controls are required for interrupting the business flow in recognition of GTS compliance blocks.

Copy-control routines in R/3 are performed by the system whenever a subsequent document is created in the business flow. These routines have rules to check the validity of creation of subsequent document; for instance, they may check customer credit limit when creating a delivery note from sales order. Similarly, when a delivery note is created, R/3 needs to check the status of the sales document in GTS. In case of a GTS compliance block for Embargo check, SPL, or Legal control, R/3 must disallow the creation of the delivery note. You need to make the following changes to the copy control routines, using transaction VOFM as follows:

```
call function '/SAPSLL/CD_STATUS_GET'
 exporting
 iv_application_level = 'SD0A'
 iv_sd_document_type = cvbak-vbtyp
 iv_sd_order_category = cvbak-auart
 iv_sd_document_number = cvbap-vbeln
 iv_sd_item_number = cvbap-posnr
 exceptions
 subsequent_process_blocked = 1
 others = 2.
 if not sy-subrc is initial.
 if v50agl-sammelgang = charx.
 perform message_handling in program (programmname)
 using cvbap-posnr
 '005'
 'E'
 '/SAPSLL/PLUGINR3'
 cvbap-posnr
 space
 space
 space.
 bp_subrc = 8.
 check 1 = 2.
 else.
```

```
perform message_handling in program (programmname)
using cvbap-posnr
'005'
'I'
'/SAPSLL/PLUGINR3'
cvbap-posnr
space
space
space.
bp_subrc = 9.
check 1 = 2.
endif.
endif.
```

After the creation of a delivery document in R/3, it is possible for the corresponding customs document in GTS to be blocked for a compliance check. For instance, the ship-to address can be changed in a delivery note requiring an SPL check, embargo check, and license determination to be performed on the document, any of which may result in a block. To account for this possibility, it is necessary to check the status of a delivery note in GTS at some or all of stages of the warehouse activities. Add the following ABAP code check in the R/3 routine for Pick Pack and post-goods issue (PGI):

```
call function '/SAPSLL/CD_STATUS_GET'
 exporting
 iv_application_level = 'SD0B'
 iv_sd_document_type = likp-vbtyp
 iv_sd_order_category = likp-lfart
 iv_sd_document_number = likp-vbeln
 iv_sd_item_number = lips-posnr
 iv_protocol = ' '
 exceptions
 subsequent_process_blocked = 2
 others = 4.
 if not ( sy-subrc is initial ) .
 message id '/SAPSLL/PLUGINR3'
 type 'E'
 number '005' with lips-posnr
 raising error.
```

7.3   Archiving Data in GTS

Archiving data in GTS is critical to ensuring the smooth operation of the system and to preserve data needed for complying with data-retention requirements from different authorities, such as export and import declaration data for customs authorities. For example, in the U.S. you are required to keep AES declaration records available for at least five years.

There are predefined archiving objects available in GTS that remove data from GTS tables associated with that object. For instance, SPL-screening audit logs are created and written to GTS tables every time SPL screening occurs. These audit-log tables can build up a lot of data over time that can slow down the system performance. GTS provides archiving object SPL_AT for archiving audit log tables. The archiving process can be used to write the data to offline storage and delete it from GTS tables. Doing so can remove data not needed in the system, resulting in improved performance, while still having it available offline if required for compliance with data-retention rules.

GTS uses the archiving framework that is used by all other SAP applications including R/3 and CRM. Transaction SARA is used to do customizing setups, create variants for data selection for archiving, and for triggering the jobs that archive data.

7.3.1   Archiving Customizing and Jobs

Transaction SARA can be used to do object-specific customizing (see Figure 7.3), which includes the following:

- Specifying the logical file that the archived data is written to
- Variants needed for the archive delete program
- Maximum size limitation for the archive file

You need to create variants that limit the data selected for archiving (see Figure 7.4). Depending on the data-retention rules for that object, you would need to exclude data that cannot be moved to offline storage or deleted.

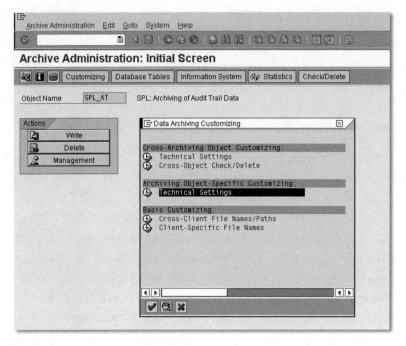

Figure 7.3 Archiving Transaction SARA

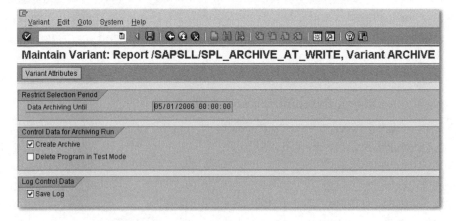

Figure 7.4 Variant for SPL Audit Log Archiving

After setting up the archive selection variants, you can run archiving jobs that write the data to an offline file and delete the data from GTS tables, taking into account the restrictions placed by the variant.

Transaction SARA also has functionality to look at past archiving jobs for the archiving object, including job details and the name of the physical files that hold the data archived from GTS tables, as seen in Figure 7.5.

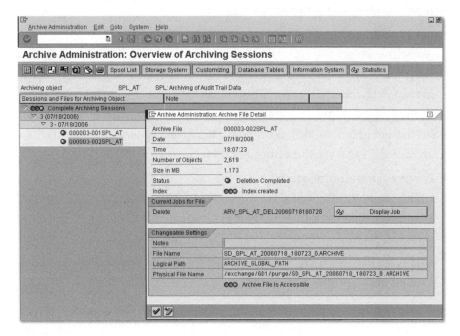

Figure 7.5 Archiving Sessions Information in Transaction SARA

7.3.2 GTS-Specific Archiving Objects

GTS-specific archiving objects archive data from the GTS application tables. The archiving object groups together application tables that hold data related to that object. The objects available in GTS are listed and explained below:

▶ **Sanctioned Party List Audit Trail Data**
Archiving object SPL_AT includes audit logs that are created during SPL screening of business partners and documents, including manual screening and comments entered while removing SPL blocks.

▶ **Sanctioned Party List Master Data**
Archiving object SPL_MD includes the SPL master data against which SPL checks are performed

- **Customs Documents and Customs Shipments**
  Archiving object CUHD includes GTS tables that hold customs documents and shipments and all their associated attributes including document partners and assigned licenses..

- **Customs Document Logs**
  Archiving object BC_SBAL includes tables that hold the log of services performed on a customs document or shipment. For instance, when license determination is performed on a customs document, GTS saves the log of messages showing date time of determination, ECCN, and license assigned to the document. BC_SBAL object can be used to archive the log from the associated tables.

- **Preference Determination**
  Archiving object PRFCALC can be used to archive data related to preference-determination runs and their associated tables.

- **Business Partners**
  Archiving object CA_BUPA can be used to archive business partners not needed in the production system.

You can also use transaction SLG2 to delete logs of data transfer from a back-end R/3 system to GTS. When business partners, products master, and documents are transferred from R/3, GTS keeps a log of both errors and successful transfer. These logs are useful for troubleshooting problems but do not meet any legal data-retention requirements. Thus, they can be deleted instead of archived, using transaction SLG2.

7.4 GTS 7.0 Versus 3.0

In GTS 7.0, a number of improvements have been made to GTS 3.0 functionality. New functionality has also been added. Some of the changes can be discussed now.

7.4.1 Compliance Management

Improvements and new functionality in the area of compliance management are given in the following sections.

Integration with Financial Accounting

Integration with financial accounting has been added to GTS 7.0 SPL screening functionality. This enables SPL screening of financial accounting business partners and related payment transactions. Included also is the ability to screen notes to the payee. This functionality is especially useful for financial institutions for complying with obligations under the U.S. Patriot Act for monitoring financial crimes and terrorist financing.

Integration with mySAP HR

Integration with mySAP HR enables you to transfer personnel data to GTS for SPL screening of your own employees. This functionality enables companies to perform due diligence expected under compliance laws to make sure none of their employees are persons on the denied-party lists.

7.4.2   Customs Management

Improvements and new functionality in the area of customs management are discussed in the sub-sections that follow.

Bonded Warehousing

A new functionality in GTS 7.0 supports bonded warehouses. Bonded warehouses are customs-authorized warehouses that allow importers to import duty-unpaid goods into the bonded warehouse for storage or further processing. Goods can either be re-exported or released for free circulation on payment of duties.

GTS 7.0 works with the R/3 feeder system to support both inbound and outbound goods movement from the bonded warehouse. Goods receipt in the feeder system can be used to trigger receipt of duty-unpaid goods into a bonded warehouse. Similarly, goods issue from the feeder system can be used to trigger an export declaration or transit declaration. Goods issue can also be used to release the goods from bonded warehouse into free circulation with the payment of customs duties on the stock.

New Customs Documents

As of GTS 7.0, the following customs documents are now available for printing:

- ▸ Customs Import/Export declarations (EU)
- ▸ Incomplete export declaration (EU)
- ▸ Canada customs coding form
- ▸ Certificate of Origin (JP)
- ▸ Local clearance notification
- ▸ Scrapping list for declaring scrapping from bonded warehouse

The following forms have been changed to reflect changes to customs forms or because of legal changes:

- ▸ NAFTA: Certificate of Origin
- ▸ MX: Certificate of Origin
- ▸ U.S.: Certificate of Origin
- ▸ U.S.: Entry Summary (CF 7501)
- ▸ U.S.: Immediate Entry (CF 3461)
- ▸ U.S.: Inward Cargo Manifest (CF 7533)
- ▸ EU: Loading List for the Single Administrative Document

7.4.3 Risk Management

Let's now examine new functionality in the area of Risk Management, which is the *Letter-of-credit* functionality. This has been added to the Risk Management module to enable import and export processes requiring a letter of credit to minimize financial risk to your company. As an exporter, a letter of credit is required by your company from customers that pose a payment risk. Your customers furnish a letter of credit, which is a guaranty involving banks in the customer's country and your country, guaranteeing payment on receipt of goods by your customer.

GTS 7.0 lets you specify customers that require letter of credit and maintain guaranties in the system. Export transactions involving a letter of credit customer are checked against the security to make sure there is available value, and documents failing this check are blocked.

7.5   Conclusion

This concludes our discussion of GTS. We discussed in this final chapter a variety of topics that are important for a successful implementation and to get the most out of your company's investment in GTS. SPL-screening your business partners in non R/3 system is important from a compliance point of view; to that end, we talked about how to screen business partners in non-R/3 systems. It is also important to have a strategy for archiving old data from GTS for performance reasons, and we talked about how to do that. If you are already on GTS 3.0, you now have learned about new functionality in GTS 7.0 that might encourage you to upgrade your existing system.

From the discussions in this book, you can see that GTS is a comprehensive global-trade-management application that covers a broad swath of trade-related issues. We talked about SAP GTS and its role in a corporation's suite of applications, the global trade trends that drive adoption of an application like GTS, and the migration path that SAP provides to existing R/3 customers to implement GTS We talked about the importance of the organizational structure setup in GTS and its mapping to the back-end R/3 structure, and the technical connection steps required for GTS to work with the back-end R/3 system.

In the area of trade compliance, we talked about the three GTS services for SPL-screening, embargo check, and license determination. These services are the basis for all compliance functions in GTS. We covered the business context and the implementation steps for each of these services and their interaction with the back-end R/3 system. Using these three services, you can monitor for compliance all aspects of your supply chain, both inbound from suppliers and outbound to customers. In the context of increased compliance focus from government agencies in response to political, proliferation and terrorism concerns, GTS can help secure your business transactions without dragging down the speed at which you execute.

The customs management discussion focused on the use of GTS to send electronic declarations to customs authorities, printing of trade documents, and the maintenance of trade-related data in GTS. We talked about the integration between R/3 and GTS that enables the electronic declarations; we also talked about the BASIS EDI functionality that is used to transmit the electronic declaration to customs offices. This functionality is important for streamlining customs-clearance procedure for your company's shipments and in some cases is a requirement for fast clearance procedures. We also talked about customs management module functionality to support paper-based customs clearance and calculation of customs duties.

In exploring the Risk Management module, we focused on how your company can use GTS makes the most of trade preference rules in NAFTA or the EU. Doing so can make your products more attractive to your customers, giving them the opportunity to claim lower import duties. We also covered restitution claims available to EU-based agricultural and processed food companies. We discussed how GTS can help those companies make the most of export refunds available to them under the EU Common Agricultural Policy.

In summary, global trade complexities are best managed by a solution like GTS that provides a centralized application working tightly with an R/3 back end to solve all your needs in the areas of compliance, customs, and risk management.

A Acknowledgements

When you reflect upon a book writing experience and wonder what drove you to write in the first place, the reasons can be simultaneously obvious and incredulous. For me, the obvious reason was the desire to share my experience implementing SAP GTS with others embarking on the same journey. The other not so obvious reason was a subliminal desire, from reading other SAP books, and the realization that I too had something to share.

I would like to acknowledge the direct and indirect contributions of those I worked with at TI during the SAP GTS implementation. They include, in no particular order: Carolyn Bettely, Sandra St. John, Chuck Pietersz, Peter Bulters, Pam Gerbsch, Chris Fowler, Harald Reiter, Ray Pechacek, Ed Pouliot and Michael Hayashiguchi. Thank you for being great partners and team mates throughout the entire process!

Dan Murphree, Kim Harrison and Joli Mallick, thank you for the opportunity, for the faith in my abilities, and for entrusting the GTS implementation to me.

Thanks to my editor Jawahara Saidullah for putting up with me and egging me on to the last mile.

And finally, I thank my wife Rosu, and my twin boys Kabeer and Arjun, for putting up with so many no fun weekends. Without your understanding and perseverance I couldn't have done it.

Jitendra Singh

B   Author Bio

Jitendra Singh has worked in various capacities in the SAP R/3 Sales and Distribution area since 1998. He led an SAP GTS implementation at Texas Instruments, Inc. and represents Texas Instruments at the ASUG GTS Influence Council. Jitendra has spoken on GTS at several conferences, including the ASUG annual conference and the ASUG SCM conference. He is the Program Chair of the ASUG SAP GTS special interest group and presents at and organizes web casts and conference sessions on GTS-related topics. Besides, GTS and R/3, Jitendra has also worked with the SAP Exchange Infrastructure. He also presented a TI customer case study at SAP TechEd. Jitendra holds an MBA from the University of Arizona and a computer science degree from India.

Index

Interested in reading more?

Please visit our Web site for all
new book releases from SAP PRESS.

www.sap-press.com